The Art of Inspiration

JERRY TOUPS, JR.

Eda Match
PUBLISHING

This book is dedicated to the thousands of former students I have taught in my three-decade-plus career that have blessed my life with an infinite amount of joy. Most importantly, it is dedicated to the possible millions of students that I will never see that will be inspired to believe in who they are by the educators that are reading and implementing the wisdom of this book in their daily classroom routine.

Contents

Prelude

Teacher assignment: write a thank you note to a teacher.
Student argument: why teachers deserve thanks

"YOU DESERVE THANKS AND HERE IS WHY...

High school is 'a school, especially in the U.S., usually including grades 9 - 12.' However, one thing they don't include in the Merriam-Webster Dictionary definition is the brutality part. It doesn't discuss the cruel wakeup call or the enormous amounts of stress buildup or the difficulty in staying motivated every day. But, what it really doesn't discuss are the teachers. They are such a huge part, and they go through the same brutality, but they have to deal with kids who are ready to revolt. However, you were never like any other teacher I had. Your energy and light made me excited to learn. While many teachers try their best to excite and motivate their students, none of them do it like you!

You are such an important part of this school. Science practically says that smiles are contagious, and even though you are not my teacher anymore, your smile still sticks with me. My friends who had you and I still say your infamous phrases and they bring back a wave of memories. Without your smile, who would be there to brighten up the school?

It is not said enough, but you deserve so much gratitude and more. Words would not be able to say my thanks to you on everything you did and still do for me. Inside school, you are an energetic, happy teacher who taught me some of my greatest life lessons. Outside of school, you are a devoted individual who is willing to drive two hours to support a student at state. [T]hat student was me. Those memories stick to me like glue, and I will always remember to believe.

While school is rough and many students would rather be home, you still deserve the happiness from that you radiate. I apologize for all the students who gave you a hard time and can't see the huge message that you are trying to express. Every day in class, I would strive to give back the positivity that you gave me. You helped me believe in myself and I wish more people saw that as your true intention, not as someone who does not care about their students.

Nevertheless, through all the hard and challenging days, you strove for better, you worked hard for others, you did your job in the absolute best way. You did that because you radiate joy, happiness, motivation, support, kindness, and most important belief. So for that and everything you do, thank you!

Pam"

SELF-REFLECTION

- What did the student say this teacher did better than the other teachers?
- What did the student say that was contagious from this teacher?
- What does the student remember about the teacher?
- What did the teacher help the student do?
- What words did the student use to describe this teacher?

- What reason did the student use to say that this teacher did their job the best way they could?

This thank you note was gifted to me by a former student. It was written after the words in this book were inked. This thank you note is perhaps the greatest testimonial evidence to the subject of this book. It is one of many student letters that are used in this book to back up the power that an inspiring teacher has over their students. A teacher that inspires their students to believe in who they are teaches amazing life lessons during the time they have with them. The purpose and goal of this book is to empower the reader to become an educator that inspires students to believe in who they are, and that by doing this, they become a source of hope to their students so they can become the best person they can be.

#AlwaysBelieve
Jerry Toups Jr.

The Art of Inspiration

~♦~

To succeed is one thing, but to make others become better through your successes is what every successful person should strive for.

In May of 1989, I started a journal called *Inspired Phrases*. This was the very first phrase I wrote in the journal. I was one year away from graduating college, and I didn't really know at that moment what career would be my calling. Decades later, this turns out to be the goal of an educator, the career my path would take me down. The *Inspired Phrases* journal that I started in 1989 is now digital and contains hundreds of phrases. I can read through these phrases and see how my career has made them come to fruition. This book will reference these phrases as we talk about ways to inspire our students.

Later that year, I made it my routine to go to Port Neches Park to do my last year of studies at Lamar University. I would usually go to this table in the evening and stay there through twilight. Watching the sunset over the Neches River, I had many moments of reflection and quiet time. I truly wanted to know why I was here. I wanted a career where I would wake up and want to go to work.

This picnic table represents "my spot." In the TV show *The Big Bang Theory*, Sheldon Cooper has said that if his life were expressed as a function in a four-dimensional Cartesian coordinate system, his spot, when he first sat on it, would be "0,0,0,0."[1] This picnic table would have the coordinates of 0,0,0,0 in my life. The moments I had at that picnic table have had profound impacts on my life and my future. When I return to "my spot," I am at total ease. My mind is clear. I leave with direction in my life.

In August of 1990, I started my career as an educator at Killeen High School. During inservice, I inked my first classroom rule as "Always Believe in Yourself." The decision to make this my first rule was the most profound of my career. This rule has been the source of inspiration for thousands of kids to BELIEVE in who they are. This book will teach the reader reproducible actions they can take to become sources of inspiration for their students. When you become a source of inspiration for students, you are reaching into their hearts in a dynamic way. You are making them feel wanted and loved. You are essentially becoming a source of hope for their future.

One day, in the spring of 1991, I was in my classroom after school having some quiet time. During this time of reflection, my past finally "clicked." The dots of my life were connected.

The Dots Of Mr. Toups' Life

5 years old	5th & 6th grade	14 years old	JH & HS	College	22 years old	23 years old
Eye injury which left me legally blind in right eye.	Verbally bullied almost daily	Father attempts suicide	friends and teachers who helped shape the choices I made	classes I had to drop which changed my career	My first summer at summer camp where I discovered my talents with kids	Accepted first job as a consumer math teacher. Made my 1st rule Always Believe in Yourself Inspiring kids to BELIEVE eventually becomes my WHY

These events forged and molded me into the adult I became.
Overcoming these valleys as a child developed the skill sets I use to thrive as a teacher.

The childhood accident at age five that left me legally blind in my right eye. The two years of school in fifth and sixth grade where I was verbally bullied and called names each day. The summer day I was at home with my sister, best friend, and dad, and my dad tried to commit suicide. The vision I have of being in my dad's room waiting for an ambulance after he shot himself is something I cannot unsee. Many of the decisions and friends I had during junior high and high school. The classes I excelled in and had to drop in college. All of these things and more directed my life and made me choose options that directed me to my career as an educator. From that moment forward, I knew my "why." The moments of quiet time at the picnic table at Port Neches Park became reality. Decades later, I would not trade my career as an educator for any other choice.

This day was a "Mount Rushmore" moment of my career. What is a Mount Rushmore moment or thing? A Mount Rushmore moment or thing is an item or event that is in the top four. You can only pick four. Later in this book, I will write about the three other Mount Rushmore' moments of my career. You will also be asked to think of Mount Rushmore items or things in your life as you journal in this book.

My career as an educator has been amazing. The moments and relationships I have with my students have generated joy and blessings and have compelled me to write this manifesto of how I have been able to teach kids to BELIEVE in who they are.

Before continuing in this book, let us do some self-reflection. Hopefully, you will form a habit of using this book as also a journal. One of the goals of this book is for the reader to have one sheet of paper used as a reference for everyday reflection to empower them to become a source of inspiration. Try to get in the habit of having a pen handy when you read this book to write down your responses. The sheet of paper generated at the end of this book will hopefully become a game changer in your career as an educator.

SELF-REFLECTION

Why did you begin your career as an educator (for those who are just starting their careers), or why have you stayed in education (for those who have continued their careers in education)?

I have had to answer this question many times during staff development meetings and teacher in-services. It is a good question to ask if you are burning out or losing the passion you once had in your career as an educator.

However, the most important "why" in education is, "Why are the kids in your classroom?" In all my years as an educator, I have never been asked this question in a training session. Write down or think of your response to "Why are the kids in your classroom?"

After reading through this book, your answers to these two questions just might change. Most, if not all, teachers have never had training in the power of nonverbal communication skills. Your nonverbal communication techniques generate the climate of your classroom. Teachers who excel at nonverbal communication have classrooms where positivity and love can be felt when one enters the room. The classroom feels different. The kids know they are loved just the way they are. When used effectively, your power to inspire students as an educator will take on new dimensions. When you inspire students with the nonverbal techniques found in this book, your influence and relations with the students will result in your career producing joy. Your students will remember lifelong lessons from your room unrelated to your academic content. You will change their lives for the better.

Mr. Toups
You have taught me to Always Believe! And I will never forget that. I hate the subject of math, but I really love your class and I will really miss you in high school. You have taught me a lot of life lessons and you have taught me most of all to never stop believing and to do things with MORE POWER. You will always have a spot in my heart.
<3 Ashley

The note above is just an example of dozens, if not hundreds, of notes I have received at the end of the year as students leave my room for summer vacation. I keep these letters in a large plastic container. If I ever have a down-and-out day, just reading through these letters will get me back on track. You will read many of these letters in this book, as they verify the words and actions I am talking about.

I have never taught a lesson on how to "BELIEVE" and after my twentieth year of teaching I began to wonder, "How am I doing this? How am I getting these letters when I don't even teach a lesson about this?" The day I found out the answers to these questions was the second "connect the dot" moment of my life and another "Mount Rushmore" day of my career. You will read about this moment later in the book.

This book will answer three great questions from the perspective of my career.

1. What is the greatest thing an educator can do for their students?
2. What is the greatest lesson an educator can teach a child?
3. What is the ultimate goal of education in terms of the students?

Inspired Phrase 907
The verbs used to describe how you interact with others will far outweigh your words.

This book will feature many of the inspired phrases I have written. The number at the end is the numerical order of the phrases that I have been inspired to write. This phrase was written during the early stages of writing this book and is a profound truth. After reading through this book, you will learn some verbs that you will need to reproduce with nonverbal communication to become a source of inspiration.

Intrinsic vs. Extrinsic

M ost teachers have not had the opportunity to observe their coworkers for an extended period. I was blessed with this opportunity during a technology grant for which I was selected. Watching my peers teach was eye-opening and made me a better educator. Through this experience and from the decades I have been in education, the wisdom I have of classroom management is priceless. I have become a great educator in regard to classroom behavior management and I also realize that many of my coworkers have excelled at this, although they get to the same results via a different manner. The ability to manage the behavior of the kids in your classroom is essential. A new teacher who doesn't get the help and assistance to develop this management will likely have a career that doesn't last. I have taught with educators that have come over from the private sector; engineers who have retired and wanted to pursue a career in education. Many of these people had great minds and wisdom they wanted to share, yet they lacked the "people and communication skills" to convey their knowledge.

In the world of public education, we are not teaching robots. We are teaching kids with a vast array of IQs and special needs. In a single class-room of 30 students, you may have IQs ranging from 80 to above 120.

You may have students with severe ADHD and other needs that the teacher will need to know to motivate that kid to succeed. To treat each student the same way and expect the same results is a misconception, and if that misconception is not corrected, success as an educator will be fleeting.

In the TV show *The Big Bang Theory*, Sheldon Cooper is a physicist with an IQ of 187, which is at the genius level but in social skills he is child-like. In the episode "The Thespian Catalyst" (Season 4 Episode 14) [1], he is tasked with teaching a class in college, but miserably fails because he doesn't have the people and communication skills needed to succeed. He is assuming the students will soak in all the knowledge he has to offer, but they are unwilling to learn. While talking to his girlfriend, Amy Farrah Fowler, she gives some profound wisdom to Sheldon.

She says, "Have you considered improving your socialization skills, thus allowing you to communicate more effectively with other people?"

Sheldon responds with, "Isn't that their burden? I am the person with something interesting to say."

Amy replies with an amazing response that will become a focus of this book. She says, **"Fair enough, but in its essence, teaching is a performance art. In the classroom paradigm the teacher has the responsibility to communicate as well as entertain and engage."** [1]

In the world we live in today, with instant entertainment and engagement on a student's cell phone, this is a profound quote. If an educator is not as entertaining and engaging as a cell phone, they are likely to be tuned out by the student, as was the situation in Sheldon's experience, and many educators who come in from the private sector. The ability to entertain and engage is primarily produced through inspiration via nonverbal communication, the subject of this book.

Now let's look at the most common ways a classroom can be managed by an educator. The primary ways a teacher can manage behavior involves motivating the students to act in a desired manner. The two main ways to motivate people are through intrinsic and extrinsic motivation. If you go to a classroom and the teacher is giving away a Skittle every time a positive action is produced by a student, they are using extrinsic motivation. A teacher using intrinsic motivation is most likely using inspiration to produce the desired actions.

If you go to www.askanydifference.com and do a search for *intrinsic vs. extrinsic,* you will find this explanation: "The difference between intrinsic and extrinsic motivation is the way an individual gets them. An individual gets intrinsic motivation from within, or by pursuing something you like, and when a person doesn't emphasize the reward they might get after completing a certain activity, on the other hand, an individual gets extrinsic motivation when they do an activity to gain something and when they do it for gaining a reward."[2]

If you are blessed to observe other educators teach, you will likely observe these three things, or a combination of them.

1. A teacher using extrinsic motivation is likely to have classroom rules with a series of DO NOTs. The students are driven to behave in fear of the consequences of breaking a rule. The room may feel cold, and you could sense friction and tension. The teacher may also be handing out rewards for good behaviors. There could be a good behavior chart in the room with consequences for students advancing or declining their position on the chart. The key feature of this room is that the students are driven to behave and learn due to an external reward or negative consequence.

2. A teacher using intrinsic motivation is likely to use positive reinforcement. The students' behavior and learning is generated through the passion the teacher exhibits for the subject content and the individual students. The room will feel quite different from an extrinsic room. You can actually sense love and positivity. In some instances, the room will feel peaceful. It is a profound experience to be in a room like this. The vibe and aura generated in this room is hard to describe, but it is a real situation. Principals and educators who have been in a room like this know what I am writing

about. This room climate is generated primarily through inspiration.

3. If the teacher cannot manage the students, learning is not happening with every student. Behind the teacher's back, the kids are misbehaving. You can sense the kids know they can misbehave without consequence. A teacher who can't correct this will likely not succeed and last in education.

Most educators begin their career being taught scenario one. For every action, there is a consequence. Rules are established and behavior is maintained by following consequences. A teacher who does not back up the rules without following through is likely to have trouble and their class will turn into scenario three. Many of the great educators I have worked with excelled at scenario one. Not only could they do scenario one, but eventually they morphed their classroom into a mode of scenario two.

Unfortunately, due to my childhood experiences, I am not a "crack the skull" disciplinarian teacher. I have a hard time handing out negative consequences. I am positive to the extreme. After decades of being an educator, I have fully developed the skills to begin the year with scenario two and develop intrinsically motivated students.

Let's continue to look at some differences of intrinsic vs extrinsic motivation in this table.[3]

INTRINSIC	EXTRINSIC
1. A person is taking up a job he/she likes to gain experience and satisfaction.	1. A person is taking up a job to earn money.
2. A person is cleaning his/her room just because he/she likes it tidy.	2. A person is cleaning up his/her room so he/she won't get punished.
3. A person is trying to study a subject because it is fascinating.	3. A person trying to study a subject to gain good scores.
4. A person participating in a sport to gain experience and enjoy it.	4. A person participating in a sport to gain rewards or prizes.
5. A person trying to contact another person to have a good time.	5. A person trying to contact a person to gain attention and personal advantage.

These examples are clear. Observe this chart and determine which of these columns is likely to produce behavior and actions that are enduring. Which column will produce relationships that are endearing and lasting?

Look especially at the second example. How many of us as adults still make our bed every day and keep our house clean through self-motivation? If your parents or guardians as a child didn't use intrinsic motivation to make you clean your room and primarily used extrinsic motivation, the consequences of this are probably evident. If you cleaned your room due to punishment consequences, once you left the house and there was no consequence for a dirty room, you probably stopped routine cleaning. Odds are you don't make your bed anymore. There is no desire to do this in your life. You probably relish the idea of not having to do the chores because you can't get punished anymore.

However, if your parents or guardians used intrinsic motivation, that value still permeates your very being. You are likely to routinely clean your house because you LIKE TO DO IT! Looking back on parenting my son (I was a single parent), I often cleaned his room with him. I made contests on who could have the best organized closet. We had fun together doing chores. To this day, my son, who is married, still cleans his house as part of his routine. It is important to him. By developing an intrinsic motivation for him to clean, I changed his life behaviors.

This is the power of generating intrinsically behaved and motivated students. A teacher who can do this and change lifelong behavior has superhero strengths. They have become a source of hope for their students. This is primarily done through inspiration via nonverbal communication.

Now let's look at the first of the three questions this book will answer. **"What is the greatest thing an educator can do for the students?"**

My answer to this question is, by the end of the year, to develop intrinsically motivated students. Teachers that do this leave their students with skills that far exceed academic ones. The students will behave and learn due to the passion generated within themselves because the teacher has inspired them. They may even choose a career in that subject matter because the teacher has inspired them intrinsically. The teacher has formed lifelong behavior changes in their students. The ability to be able to do this each year with the students in your room is humbling. As educators, we truly have careers that can change the life of a child.

Above all, if you are only using extrinsic motivation to get the desired consequences from your students, once the extrinsic motivator is removed, the behavior will likely cease, just like cleaning your bedroom.

Unfortunately, educators are usually not given training on how to produce intrinsic motivation. In my three decades plus career as an educator, the only time I have been in a training like this is when I am presenting the training that is found in this book.

So the question is, "How do you develop and generate students who behave and learn intrinsically?" I have made the following diagram to illustrate how I have generated intrinsically motivated students.

INTRINSIC LEARNING DIAGRAM

1. POSITIVE

Establish a POSITIVE classroom environment from day one. Your opening day should be captivating.

2. BELIEVE

Your students should have NO DOUBT that you BELIEVE they will succeed.
1st Classroom Rule
Always Believe in Yourself

3. LOVE

Shower you students with LOVE by POSITIVE affirmation on WHO THEY ARE, their achievements, ANYTHING that makes them special.

4. LEARNING

Once the 1st 3 steps are in place, students are likely to learn and behave INTRINSICALLY.

Before we go any further, is this 100% guaranteed to work? The answer is no. We do not go home with our students. We do not control the environment. The students have twenty-four hours a day, seven days a week. However, the consequences of following the "Intrinsic Learning Diagram" are profound. I can honestly say this works for a vast majority of the students I have been blessed to teach.

This book will follow the first three steps to create the product of an intrinsic learner. What exactly is an intrinsic learner? Intrinsic learners have "a type of motivation that involves doing things because they find them naturally satisfying or doing things for their own sake because they find them enjoyable."[4]

Just as having "Always Believe in Yourself" as your first rule, you also cannot make students learn intrinsically. So how do you create intrinsically motivated students? In the same article that is linked above, two of the prominent researchers on intrinsic motivation, Edward Deci and Richard Ryan, stated that there were three innate psychological needs for intrinsic motivation to occur:

1. A need for competence
2. A need to feel independent and autonomous
3. A need to feel connected and related to others [5]

Steps one and two are generated when the students know you believe in them, and they start believing in themselves. Step three is generated in the love part of the Intrinsic Learning Diagram.

Since 1990, my years of being an educator have shown me that creating intrinsically motivated students involves inspiration through nonverbal communication, the subject of this book. When students are inspired by their teacher's positive attitude and nonverbal communication skills, the results can be profound. There have been several years of my teaching career when during the last three weeks of school the other teachers are complaining about their kids shutting down and no longer wanting to work, yet in my class, the kids are on task and still completing their assignment. Why does this occur? The Intrinsic Learning Diagram answers the question. It all starts by making your classroom a positive climate zone that can be felt by others when they come into your room.

There are many times when college students observing my class tell me, "Your classroom feels different from the others. You are so positive with the kids." This positive climate should be created on the very first day of school, which will be the subject of the next chapter.

After your positive climate zone is established, the kids need to know that you BELIEVE in them and their ability to succeed. When you LOVE the kids for who they are, and your actions (nonverbal communication) back up your words, this will likely result in the students being intrinsically motivated in your classroom. On top of this, once they are inspired to "Always Believe," you have probably started the process of growth mindset.

The "BELIEVE" and "LOVE" part of this process are primarily achieved through your use of nonverbal communication. A process that is so powerful yet is almost always absent in the entirety of an educator's professional development career. When you can accomplish this, your career will take on a different trajectory.

Inspired Phrase 865
A teacher's inspiration in the classroom today has the potential to change the world for the better in the future.

I wrote this phrase before the process of writing this book took place. It is a powerful truth to the ability of a teacher to inspire intrinsic learners.

Positivity

This was from an anonymous junior high student.

"Mr. Toups' first classroom rule isn't a rule, it's a lifestyle. Anyone who has ever been in Mr. Toups' class cannot help but walk away changed. Everything Mr. Toups has been through and yet he still believes and is one of the most optimistic people I know. I will never give up and will always BELIEVE."

Notice the power of this student testimonial is backing up the words and actions you will learn from this book. The student realizes their life has been changed and so have those of their classmates. They also mention the impact of the teacher being optimistic. If you look at the "Intrinsic Learning Diagram" you will read this about POSITIVE. "Establish a POSITIVE classroom environment from day one. Your opening day should be captivating." Do your very best to establish the positive zone in your room from the very first day.

I remember being in college and having my professors and other guest speakers say, "Don't smile until after Christmas." I now often look back and think, "How sad." These educators missed out on half the year to create and be a source of happiness. Your smile is one of the most powerful forms of nonverbal communication you possess. It can enlighten a child's day. Your smile can be a source of hope not only for your students but also your coworkers. Your first day of school, not only should you smile, but you should make your best effort to have every single student leave your classroom with a smile as well. Be the teacher that kids go home and tell their parents about. How do you do this? Read on.

As the kids come into my room on opening day, I greet them with a smile and show them how to find their desk. While they are getting seated, they are watching a powerful video I have made of all the places I have been to. The video's audio background is the song "I've Been Everywhere" by Johnny Cash. On the paper the kids pick up as they walk into my room, they are assigned to write down two places from the video they would like to go to or to learn more about. During the year, about every three weeks, I take them on a Mr. Toups field trip in my room by showing them pictures and videos of the places I have been to. While the video is playing, I check the roll by my seating chart, so I do not have to spend my valuable time individually calling out names to check attendance.

The rest of the class period, I set the stage to tell the kids "my story" of why I do what I do. You will never have another opportunity to impact the kids like this. The first day the students are in your room is the time to empower them with the story of why you are an educator. This is the moment of your "first impression." When your students know that you love what you do, this is a huge step to the inspiration you will have over them as the school year goes on. I then tell the kids about the first memory of my life. (This story in full is the first chapter in my book, *The Story of Always Believe*.)

In summary, the summer before my kindergarten school year, I was playing ball at my neighbor's house. Through a childhood accident, a stick was thrown into my right eye, which blinded my vision in that eye. That accident had profound impacts on my future. Decisions were made, friends were kept and lost, activities were avoided, and the result was that after completing college, my choices led me into the education career. The injury also made my right eye a "lazy eye," which means that both of my eyes don't look in the same direction. This story is necessary to tell at the beginning of the first day since when I call on my students, they need to look at my left eye instead of my right eye. I end this story with humor so the kids get one of their first laughs in my room.

The importance of telling your story to the kids is immense. The more the students know about you, the more likely they will tell you about them. Tell them stories of adversities you overcame throughout your life and especially your childhood. The students need to know that adversity and tribulations are a part of life, that you once walked in their shoes, and that you were able to get through these times. Also give them the opportunity to let them tell you about them. On the first day of school, I have my students write down their first ever memory and they write down two places they would like to visit from my opening video. I start the process of learning about them from the very first day.

The next slide in my PowerPoint is for the students to learn my "favorite things." I tell them where I am from, the places I have taught, my favorite color, my favorite TV Show, my favorite sport, and my hobbies.

After I tell them these things, we then play three rounds of two truths and a lie. In two truths and a lie, you present three items about your life of which two are true and one is a lie. This is the highlight of my first day. My kids learn impactful and humorous truths about my life in a fun way. This is what the kids go home and tell their parents about. It produces a wow factor that is not easily replicated in their other classes. On the opening day form the students pick up, they are asked to share with me an example of two truths and a lie from their life.

In the remaining amount of time, I do my best to call out each student by name. When the child hears their name called, it justifies their existence in your room. When the dismissal bell rings, I make sure I am at the door. As each student leaves, I point to them and tell them, "You are awesome," with conviction. As they pass me, I tap them on the shoulder (the very beginning of non-verbal communication to each of my students). Usually, every kid has a smile on their face as they are told, "You are awesome."

You can also use your room to tell your story. My classroom walls are lined with posters featuring my inspired phrases placed on background pictures that I took from all over the USA. I also have a #ToupsPose wall that features my famous #ToupsPose at points all around the country. A USA highway map is in the middle of my #ToupsPose pictures. I have highlighted all the roads I went down. The kids really enjoy viewing the pictures and looking at the map of places I have been. During the course of the year, I share stories of the places I have been to and relate the places to their history class.

Remember, use the opening day to tell your story to your kids. This is the only chance at your first impression with them. Do your best to make this a day they will not forget. As the year goes on, learn each of your kids' stories. The more the kids know about you, the more likely they are to tell you about them. The more you know about each other, the more impact your nonverbal communication will have. Your relationships with the kids will take on a dynamic that will truly be life changing.

So begins my journey with my students that ends with them being intrinsically motivated learners and being inspired to BELIEVE they can succeed.

Watch Mr. Toups' opening virtual day lesson.

PUT IT INTO ACTION

What slide show could you be showing as your kids come into your class on day one?

Write out at least one set of two truths and a lie about you.

Truth:

Truth:

Lie:

Inspired Phrase 490
Great teachers form relationships that last a lifetime.

This phrase is yet another goal of this book. After you learn how to inspire your students, you will form memories that will last the lifetime of your students.

Always Believe

While still in college, I wrote the fifteenth inspired phrase.

Inspired Phrase 15
The first step toward succeeding is believing in yourself and your abilities.
The first step toward defeat is doubting yourself and your abilities. Always
believe in yourself and success will occur often.

In January 1990 I wrote "always believe in yourself" for the first time. Later that August, while in inservice of my first year of teaching, I decided to make my first classroom rule "Always Believe in Yourself." This was the greatest decision of my career. Since that moment, my career has been themed on inspiring kids to believe in who they are, even though I am academically teaching them mathematics.

The power of believing in yourself is immense. Andrew Shorten writes, "Arguably, absolutely everything you have in your life is a result of you believing it is possible."[1] He continues, "Believing in yourself creates more opportunities and more happiness. Meanwhile, experiencing more success and having a richer life makes you more confident in what you can achieve."[2]

Growth mindset is also empowered when you believe in yourself. Tony Robbins writes,

> The Association for Psychological Science studied brain activity to observe what happens when someone makes a mistake. Researchers observed one reaction when participants realized they'd made a mistake, and a second when they went to fix the mistake. After, they asked the participants what they'd learned from their errors. Here is where knowing how to believe in yourself came into play: Participants who believed they could learn from their mistakes improved their performance on tasks they completed after they made the mistake. This is called having a growth mindset, and it's essential to believing in yourself.[3]

You could say that to start believing in yourself, you must develop a growth mindset to believe you can succeed. Or, that when you learn to believe in yourself that you have developed a growth mindset. Inspiring someone to develop this growth mindset is a key to unlocking academic improvement. This happens when the student starts believing in their talents. A child is likely to start believing in themselves when an adult in their life believes in them more than they do. I have personally seen this take place in my career.

In my 894th Inspired Phrase, I wrote: "When you believe, impossible becomes just an opinion." On a trip recently to Disney World, I saw a quote from Walt Disney which said, "It's kind of fun to do the impossible."[4] Disney believed in the ground-breaking products and innovations he was thinking of and his belief made them become reality.

Through my career of watching kids learn to believe in who they are in my classroom, I have seen the following take place:

- Believing in yourself will eventually conquer your self-doubts.
- Believing in yourself is the first step to achieving your goals.

As an educator who has centered his career on inspiring his students to believe in who they are, these are also truths that I have seen played out in my classroom.

- Keep telling others to believe and eventually they will.
- If you tell a child to believe and you back your words with actions that motivate them, they will likely overcome the odds.
- Success is accelerated when the pupil knows the teacher believes in them.
- A child taught to believe can motivate others to succeed.
- If a student knows the teacher believes in them, their learning plateau grows exponentially.
- And lastly, believing in yourself is the keystone of your very being.

The second question this book is themed around is, "What is the greatest lesson an educator can teach a child?"

The following student testimonial letters will answer that question.

"Dear Mr. Toups, Thank you for being such a wonderful and influencing teacher. I will never forget all the things you taught me. So when I go to college I will still remember my 8th grade math teacher who showed me that he cared and that if I believe in myself I can do anything. PS Always Believe" - Angela

"Always Believe In Yourself. This phrase will always stick with me. Throughout the year, there have been times where I just wanted to quit math, but I would remember what you told us. ALWAYS BELIEVE. Now I don't just use this saying in math class. I use it on every task I can possibly think of. I also tell other people when they believe they can accomplish a task. You are the best teacher ever and have a great life." - Anonymous student

"I think we should always believe in ourselves because if we don't, we will not succeed in life. I have put myself down and lost so many times, but because of you, Mr. Toups, I'm always going to see the positive side of things and always believe." -Anonymous student

"Always believe in myself is very important to me because it actually worked! I went into this class thinking I was going to fail and get kicked out. Mr. Toups told us to believe, and the more I understood what I was doing, the more I believed in myself. He always believed in me, which really helped me pass this class. I know that if I keep this attitude that there ain't nothing I can't do! Thank you, Mr. Toups! Love Brianna! Always Believe" -Brianna

Through these letters, you can see that when an educator inspires a student to believe in who they are, it transcends their being. They not only believe they can succeed in the subject you are teaching, but they also use that belief to help them in other areas of life.

What is the most important lesson an educator can teach a student?

This is the second question this book answers. *I firmly believe the greatest lesson you can teach a child is to believe in who they are.* I have seen the consequences of doing this in my career and how it empowers my students to succeed, not just in my subject of math, but in life itself.

Inspired Phrase 333
To enable someone to believe they can be successful just might be the single most important lesson in their life.

I wrote this after two decades in my career. Over time, you can watch your former students grow up and succeed as adults. This is powerful. When, as adults, these students are still appreciative of the belief you instilled in them when they were students, it is simply overwhelming. This is done through inspiration. How do you develop the skills to empower students with inspiration? Keep on reading.

Inspiration

Inspiring others is a key to teaching kids to learn and behave intrinsically, and inspiration is a powerful ally when teaching kids to have faith in who they are and believing they can succeed. This student letter acknowledges the power of inspiration.

"Always believe in yourself inspires me because you inspire me to always believe. You are my inspiration for the goals that I have now and the ones that I will have later in life. You made me see that there is always a reason to keep going and believing! I will miss you! Love, Tiffy"

When kids know that you, as an adult, believe in who they are more than they do, the consequences are immense, as you can see in the above letter. "You are the inspiration for the goals I have now and the ones I will have later in life." This, in its essence, is HOPE! Giving kids hope is yet another side effect of developing inspiration in your classroom.

You may be asking yourself, what is inspiration? Inspiration can have a variety of meanings, from a spiritual aspect to an artistic aspect, and to even writing, like my inspired phrases and even parts of this book.

Here are some definitions of inspiration from a variety of sources.[1][2]

- To impel, spur, or motivate someone.
- To make someone feel that they want to do something and can do it.
- To feel with courage or strength of purpose.
- Fill someone with the urge or ability to do or feel something.
- To influence, move, or guide by divine or supernatural action.
- To fill with an animating, quickening, or exalting influence.
- To affect, guide, or arouse by divine influence.
- To fill with enlivening or exalting emotion.

In the article "5 Proven Ways to Inspire People to Be Great" by Tony Robbins, he states, "When you know how to inspire others, you create impactful relationships."[3]

How many professional developments have you been to that have told you teaching is all about the relationships then they never tell you how to do this? I would say I have heard this over a dozen times and then sit there waiting for the presenter to tell the other teachers in the room how to succeed at this. I can honestly say that after three decades of being in education, I have never been in a workshop or seminar that teaches the concepts found in this book. But learning how to inspire our kids is the building block to building the impactful relationships that are mentioned by Tony Robbins.

I can also add that when researching this book, most inspirational topics I found were focused on the business world. There was little literature on how educators can learn to inspire their students, which might simply be the greatest skill an educator can learn. Inspiring a student is one of the greatest ways to develop self-esteem, self-confidence, and establishing a growth mindset of "I can." Educators learning how to do this, and then replicating these actions in their classes will change the lives of their students for the better.

Tony Robbins continues in his article,

> Mastering how to inspire others hinges on leadership skills which evoke feelings of awe and wonder in others. In fact, learning how to inspire people and influence them distinguishes great leaders from mediocre ones. The answer is straightforward: Since every person on Earth is influenced by his or her thoughts, feelings, and behaviors, true leaders make skillful use of those "pressure points" to influence others' behaviors.[4]

For those in education who have been blessed to observe teachers in action, they can see and feel great educators in their classrooms. Great educators know the art of inspiration. Their room is a beacon of positivity. The kids know they are safe and loved in the room. Intrinsic behavior is evident. I wish every educator had the opportunity to see the difference between an inspiring teacher and a teacher who has built their success on extrinsic motivation. The classes feel and look totally different, as I described in the chapter over intrinsic vs extrinsic.

Tony Robbins continues in his article and states five steps in which leaders can inspire others. Remember, most literature I found on inspiration is about the workplace and not in education, but these five steps are evident in this book.

1. Lead by example
2. Set goals and expectations that inspire employees
3. Master empathy
4. Focus on relationships
5. Embrace the process[5]

Steps 1, 3, and 4 will be discussed later in this book. Step 2 is pretty clear. When you set your first classroom rule as "Always Believe in Yourself," that is a very inspiring goal for every student. Who doesn't want to learn and have faith to believe in who they are? When you theme your classroom around this, you are doing step five, which is to embrace the process.

In 1990, during my first week of teacher in-service, I really had no idea of the impact "Always Believe in Yourself" would have on my students—both in the classroom and even later in their life. I also had no idea of the impact it would have on me. It is now my passion and desire, it is my why, to share the power of inspiring kids to believe in who they are to other educators.

Michael Angier has written his "Top Ten Ways to Inspire Others to Be Their Best." Remember, these steps are written for the business world, but can also work in a classroom setting. These steps are also found in the writings of this book. Michael Angier says his top ten steps are...

1. Be a good example
2. Care about others
3. Encouragement
4. Be inspired yourself
5. Share from your own experience
6. Be vulnerable
7. Tell stories
8. Be a good communicator
9. Challenge people
10. Read[6]

Let's go through these steps in terms of an educational setting. Notice the first step Angier mentions is also the same as Robbins. It is important to be the example you want your students to be. If you want your students to believe in who they are, you must believe in them more than they believe in themselves. You must also role model the actions you want your students to behave like, which will be talked about later in this book.

Step two is to care about others. This is basically empathy, another topic in the future reading of this book.

Step three is encouragement, which goes back to the educator believing in the child.

Step four is for you to be inspired. This stems from knowing your "why." In the book *Define Your Why*, Barbara Bray gives detailed step-by-step activities on how to know your "why." If you are going to work each and every day just to collect a paycheck, the students will know this. When you are able to know your "why" you will develop a passion for being at work. This passion is the P in PIRATE from *Teach Like a Pirate* written by Dave Burgess. Teachers who are passionate about their work and are inspired to be at work, will in turn inspire their students.

Steps five, six, and seven mean for you to let your students know you walked in their shoes. The happy memories of childhood are the treasure chests of life, but when kids are going through the valleys of tribulation in their childhood, this is scary. They haven't had the wisdom of life to know they will be defined and forged in the valleys of life. This is where empathetic and caring adults in their life come in. As an educator, if you are able to share stories of your childhood and let the kids know you walked in their shoes through the valleys, this will create inspiration. It will produce hope in the students. I wrote my first book, *The Story of Always Believe* to do this. The first three stories in this book talk about the three deepest valleys of my childhood. A student reading this book, then knowing how I overcame them and inspired them as an adult, sees me in a different light. The "relationship" I have built with that child goes to the next level. They will likely begin to behave and learn intrinsically in my room, and they will start believing in their abilities.

Step eight talks about communication. Great minds have desired to become teachers to share their knowledge with the kids, only to leave the profession due to their lack of behavior management skills. Likewise, people who have profound people skills won't succeed due to a lack of knowledge and ability to communicate the aspects of the academic curriculum. It is essential for an educator to know their academic learning objectives and be able to fluently communicate them. Failure to be able to do this will have devastating results.

Step nine is to challenge people. This directly goes to having high expectations for the kids. The kids will know what the teacher wants from them and will perform to that level. Experienced educators will verify this to new teachers.

Step ten is to read. Never ever be content at your levels as an educator. Always desire to become better. THERE IS NO STATUS QUO IN THE PROFESSION OF EDUCATION. You are either improving or decreasing in your abilities. Hopefully through reading this book, you will increase your capabilities to motivate and teach your students to a new level.

In another business article "8 Things the Smartest Leaders Do to Motivate Their Employees," Marcel Schwantes writes, "Science has found that positive emotions are at the root of human motivation. It's how employees 'feel' that will drive motivation deep within them."[7]

This goes back to an educator's success determining how they make the students "feel" in their classroom. As stated earlier, we are told as educators to make the kids feel wanted and loved in our classroom, but yet, it is assumed we know how to do this. Later in this book, you will learn how to make students feel so that inspiration is produced.

The steps Schwantes creates are clearly for a business world, but the impacts of doing this in an educational environment will also work. His eight steps are...

1. Schedule more one-on-one time
2. Find out what motivates them
3. Provide the resources they need to do their work exceptionally well
4. Praise and compliment them often
5. Help co-create purposeful work
6. Help them develop new skills
7. Actively involve them
8. Believe in them[8]

Again, let's look at these steps from a teacher's perspective. Steps one and two go to having individual time with each and every student.

Getting to know them as individuals, not just as a name on the seating chart. Kids will know when you are trying to get to know who they are. This in turn will generate inspiration.

Step three goes back to your curriculum. As a team of educators at your campus, you truly need to work together to make sure your students have access to curriculum that will make them excel academically.

Step four refers to the section of this book about positivity.

Step five stresses to make sure the students know their voices are heard. Let them help you generate questions and involve them in the process of your class and subject.

Step six is hopefully the outcome of succeeding in your academic learning objectives. Step six, developing new skills, is a real goal of the educational process.

Step seven empowers your student voice in your room. If you are involving the students in the learning process, they are likely to be inspired to achieve.

And lastly, step eight. BELIEVE IN THEM. Even in the business world, employees want to know their bosses believe in them. Making your first rule "Always Believe in Yourself" and then inspiring your students to succeed at this will have monumental consequences for their future. In the book *Dare to Inspire* by Allison Holzer, Sandra Spataro, and Jen Grace Baron, the topic of inspiration is taken to the psychological level. They write,

> We define the initial moment of inspiration - the spark - as the intersection of possibility and invincibility. Possibility expands the boundary of what could be, it extends beyond our normal limits of what is possible or current conceptions of what may "work." Possibility is firmly rooted in hope – it introduces new ways of thinking about things and a new capacity to visualize, create, analyze, and foresee. Invincibility is the confident energy that complements possibility in the spark of inspiration and translates into action. The spark of inspiration can transform our mindsets: it makes the impossible seem possible. It can change how we see our own capacity; it can even change the way we see the world.[9]

The authors of *Dare to Inspire* later talk about the life story of Captain Barrington Irving, a pilot who overcame tremendous adversity as a child, who later used his skills to develop an organization to inspire young kids in the field of aviation.

> Captain Barrington Irving says that "inspiration is a common denominator," where economic status, race, and other factors disappear. "You can inspire a child to do anything," he says. When children are inspired to do something, they don't ask the question, "How much math do I have to learn to do this?" They just learn it. Children previously discouraged from learning or disinterested in the classroom suddenly show interest and are fully engaged in learning.[10]

Notice what Captain Barrington Irving says about the consequences of inspiring students. They don't ask how much learning is needed, they just learn it. This happens because the inspiration has triggered intrinsic motivation. The kids are learning because they want to learn and will overcome the challenges needed to achieve the end result. This explains how believing enough in your goals and your abilities can turn the impossible into reality.

The authors of *Dare to Inspire* continue their talk about inspiration. "Inspiration is contagious. As with your emotions, you can become inspired by others' inspiration, just as they can be inspired by yours."[11]

Later in this book the authors let us know why inspiration is contagious.

> ***"How and why is inspiration contagious? When a person feels inspired, he or she expresses these emotions through verbal or body language. People who are around an inspired person will pick up on the verbal and body language communication of inspiration and their mirror neurons will start to fire and replicate the same emotions of inspiration."***[12]

The Power of Inspiration

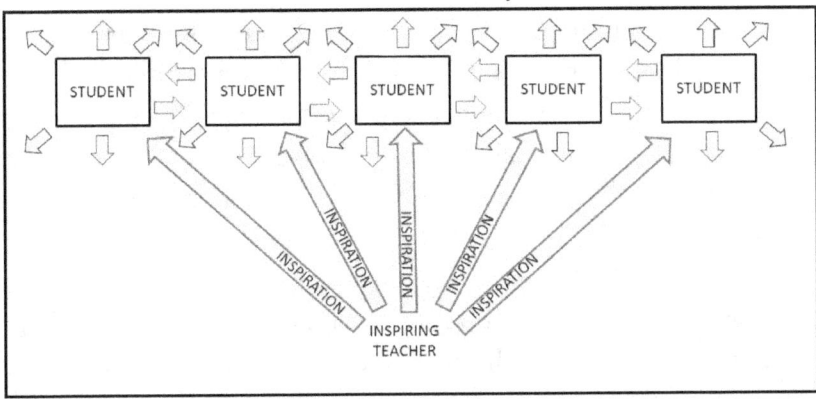

This is in essence the very heart of this book. You will inspire others through nonverbal communication skills. When you nonverbally communicate the actions that produce inspiration those around you will have psychological responses that mirror your nonverbal communication. This is why walking the talk and being an example is a very powerful source of inspiration. This is why it is said your nonverbal communication will always trump the words that you verbally communicate. If you tell someone to believe in themselves, but your actions don't back up those words, your success to inspire that person will be negated by your actions.

The authors of *Dare to Inspire* continue this fascinating process of inspiration and how people react psychologically to inspiring people, "This phenomenon occurs because humans have what is called an open limbic system: we pick up on one another's cues and are impacted emotionally by one another. From an adaptive point of view, the open limbic system and mirror neurons are what allow social bonding and trust to occur."[13]

The "mirror neurons" talked about in *Dare to Inspire* are intriguing. If you research into mirror neurons, you will find that this is a relatively new field that started in 1999 and there is little research into this subject. The discovery and the influence of mirror neurons has not been replicated in studies. The study of mirror neurons is at the heart of why we do what we do—why we feel and react to our feelings. This is different for every human being and is what makes us individuals.

It is important to remember as you read through this book, that many of the truths I share are from the bubble that is my three decade plus educational career. Every teacher will use the techniques found in the book differently. We will all replicate the verb of LOVE in different ways, because we are unique individuals with vastly different backgrounds.

A teacher's skill to impact their students emotionally through inspirational nonverbal communication skills cannot be overestimated in the success they will have with their students. Yet, how many training sessions are teachers given to perfect these skills? As stated above, these skills are at the core of building the relations with the kids that result in student growth. They are at the epicenter of generating trust and belief. A teacher perfecting these skills will transform into superhero teacher level status. This was drawn by one of my students to illustrate this.

The authors of *Dare to Inspire* continue in their explanation of how sources of inspiration occur, "What makes you distinctly great can also be a source of inspiration. Both Dr. Chris Peterson and Dr. Martin Seligman, pioneering researchers in the field of positive psychology, have studied how people use their character strengths to make a positive impact in the world. In their research, they have found twenty-four distinct character strengths that are consistently valued across cultures as virtuous attributes, such as creativity, kindness, hope, love of learning, and fairness.[14] People who use one or more of their character strengths in their work, regularly tend to be more engaged and have greater well-being at work."[15]

The character strengths talked about in this quote are critical in nonverbal communication skills. **These character strengths and the ability to reproduce them nonverbally are at the heart of inspiring students.** Notice they say these character strengths are consistently valued across cultures as virtuous attributes, and some of them are creativity, kindness, hope, love of learning, and fairness. In my first year of teaching, in the spring of 1991, coincidentally I made it my goal for my students to describe me with some of these "virtuous attributes." The consequences of that goal have been enormous in my life and have empowered me to thrive in my career as an educator.

Inspired Phrase 907
The verbs used to describe how you interact with others will far outweigh your words.

We are about to discuss the verbs that educators should strive to replicate.

Mount Rushmore Moment Two

~~~

Remember earlier in the book talking about "Mount Rushmore" moments? A Mount Rushmore event or thing is in the top four of that classification. If you teach history, having your kids list their Mount Rushmore of famous presidents will lead to great conversations. The kids can only pick four, but they must back up their four choices. The passion behind the choices will become evident in their conversations. Kids may even "inspire" their friends to change their choices because of their passion.

In the opening chapter I talked about the first Mount Rushmore day of my career as an educator. It happened in the spring of my first year teaching in 1991. That afternoon in a powerful series of visions of my past, the dots of my life were connected. This is the day I knew my "why." From that day forward my career became my passion. Also remember, people who are passionate have the power of inspiration. Knowing your "why" when you go to work is almost essential to becoming a consistent force of inspiration for your students.

The second Mount Rushmore moment happened in the Spring of 2018 at a Gifted and Talented update workshop. I was in the process of writing my first book, *The Story of Always Believe*. At the end, I wanted to make a section on how I was able to teach my students to "Always Believe." My students often gifted me letters at the end of the year as they left for summer break. Many of these letters were thanking me for teaching them to always believe. Yet, I wasn't teaching any lessons on how to believe. I was puzzled and perplexed. I wanted to let other educators know how I was succeeding at teaching kids to always believe when I wasn't even teaching them to do this.

At the Gifted and Talented update, the presenter, a Texas A&M professor, was amazing. I thought, "She may know how I am teaching my students to believe."

Before lunch I went up and showed her pictures of me, my students, and my classroom. I shared with her strengths about my career and asked her if she knew how I was able to teach my kids to believe. After looking through my pictures and hearing my story, she said, "You have profound nonverbal communication skills. Your nonverbal communication skills will always carry more weight than your spoken words. You are teaching these kids to believe through nonverbal communication."

That set my brain twirling. I remember my college speech professor actually discussing nonverbal communication in my freshman year in college. I went to lunch and while eating I began to research nonverbal communication on my smartphone. The results were enormous. I thought, "I actually do all of this." I had no idea of these skills and the impact they were having on my students. These nonverbal communication skills were developed over the course of my career to get my students to behave and be successful. Essentially the nonverbal skills were being replicated by my students, possibly through mirror-neurons, and were forming intrinsic behavior and learning. These same nonverbal communication skills are at the heart of the inspiration involved in teaching the kids to always believe.

A few months later, and after my first book was finalized for publication, I remembered back in time to my first-year teaching. After school each day I had quiet reflection time. It was in the spring of 1991 when my first Mount Rushmore even happened. Later that spring I made it my goal for my students to describe me with these words: love, joy, peace, kindness, gentleness, goodness, patience, and faithfulness. These are indeed the Fruits of the Spirit as written by the apostle Paul in the book of Galatians. Each morning for the first few years of my career I would read these words over and over.

Then the spark of inspiration hit me.

I have been nonverbally communicating these words into existence.

By nonverbally communicating these words (love, joy, peace, kindness, goodness, gentleness, faithfulness, and patience), I have become a source of inspiration. These words, and replicating them, have been the very key to the successes I have had as an educator.

That moment was the second connect the dot moment I have had in my career as an educator and is the reason I am writing this book. It was the second Mount Rushmore moment of my career. I know my nonverbal skills can be replicated to produce similar results by other educators with different kids. My desire is for this book to impact educators and students with these skills.

Even greater, when reading through the letters that my students have gifted me, I discovered something. The students were using many of these words in describing their experiences in my classroom. You will read many of these letters later in this book. They are profound testimonials to the words I am writing.

As mentioned in the previous section of this book, people who replicate distinct character traits that are consistently valued across cultures as virtuous attributes become sources of inspiration.[1] (13 on page 33) They are generating psychological responses in those around them to replicate their actions. My ability to nonverbally communicate love, joy, peace, kindness, goodness, gentleness, patience, and faithfulness to my kids is at the core of my ability to inspire thousands of kids to believe in who they are.

From now on in the context of this book we will define love, joy, peace, kindness, goodness, gentleness, patience, and faithfulness as the "ultimate teacher descriptors."

When your students begin to describe who you are with these words, your career and your life will take a different trajectory.

Inspired Phrase 885
A teacher's inspiration in the classroom today has the potential to change the world for the better in the future.

Your ability to reproduce the "ultimate teacher descriptors" can have a powerful effect on your students' futures.

Nonverbal Communication

"Mr. Toups

Thank you so much for being such a great role model and inspiration to this community. You've always believed in everyone, and the support you provide to this school is beyond recognition. Thank you so much for teaching the next generation of leaders, not just math, but also how to be a great person in life.

All things are possible if you believe."

— ANONYMOUS PARENT LETTER

Steps two and three in the "Intrinsic Learning Diagram," BELIEVE and LOVE, are accomplished through nonverbal communication.

Before we get to the "ultimate teacher descriptors" we need to talk about what exactly is nonverbal communication? Your skills to use nonverbal communication with your students result in your influence going beyond your classroom walls, as evident in the above parent letter. Write down some words that would describe the nonverbal communication skills that a successful teacher would have.

Write down some words that would describe an unsuccessful teacher's nonverbal communication skills.

Some of you may have written down these words: eye contact, open body language, closed body language, smile, frown, sneer, happy, sad, well-dressed, poorly dressed, cold, warm, and many others.

As the Texas A&M professor told me, "Your nonverbal communication will always trump your verbal communication." Your students will describe who you are by your non-verbal communication. These words are adjectives but, in reality, they are verbs that you do, which in turn becomes the words people describe who you are. They are the words that generate how you make others feel about themselves. As it is often said, "A student will not remember the content you teach them, but they will remember the way you made them feel."[1] The way you make them feel is done through nonverbal communication.

Nonverbal communication can be defined as – "the process of conveying meaning without the use of words either written or spoken. In other words, any communication made between two or more persons using facial expressions, hand movements, body language, postures, and gestures."[2]

Nonverbal communication is at the center of maintaining and establishing the emotional aspects of a relationship. It is the actions of your body that back up your words. If you tell the kids that they are amazing, but your actions do not back up these words, the kids will know your words are meaningless. However, when your actions reinforce the words of love you tell the kids, you will impact the kids and make them "feel" approved. Remember, your nonverbal communication will always trump your verbal communication. You can direct students through verbal communication, but if you learn to direct behavior through nonverbal communication, you will inspire them and generate behavior that is intrinsically motivated. A teacher who can inspire children to correctly act intrinsically has taught their children life lessons far beyond the content of the curriculum. They are teaching kids essential life skills through their actions that can be described with verbs. They are walking the talk and the kids notice this. This is "Being the example" that was referred to earlier in this book on how companies can inspire employees.

A teacher's use of nonverbal communication to create intrinsic learners is one of the most powerful tools in a teacher's tool belt, yet teachers are seldom if ever taught how to utilize nonverbal communication to accomplish this. One reason why is that all educators are unique individuals. We will connect and inspire kids through the same philosophy, but with a unique skill set. You are about to learn reproducible actions that will use your unique skill set to accomplish this.

Inspired Phrase 478
Your actions and words should encourage and inspire others to do good.

When students begin to describe who you are with the "ultimate teacher descriptors" they will begin to replicate your actions. You will be inspiring them to do good.

Ultimate Teacher Descriptors

"Mr. Toups

I have loved your class and I will miss you. Even when I feel down, I come to this class, and I realize that this is like my home. I feel hope in this classroom. I feel like this is the end of the best part of my life. You are an amazing teacher! I will remember everything you taught me, especially the first classroom rule! I will always believe!

Goodbye, sadly

—Michelle "

This student letter is another example of the letters you will continue to read through this book that are testimonies to the words I am writing. During my career I have had students write letters and draw pictures in which these "ultimate teacher descriptors" are used. When kids describe who you are with these words, your influence on them becomes dynamic. You will change their lives. You will become a source of hope. You will be a force of goodness to all those around you. This will become evident as you read the students letters that are found throughout this book.

Little did I realize back in August 1990 when I made my first classroom rule "Always Believe in Yourself," then later in the spring of 1991 when I made it my goal to be described with the ultimate teacher descriptors, how potent the combination of these two things would become on the students I was and would be teaching in my career. This all became clear to me when the Texas A&M professor told me I had "profound nonverbal communication skills." These descriptors are indeed replicated by nonverbal communication, a skill that is seldom, if ever, taught to educators.

The research behind inspiration is little and far between. Remember, as previously referenced, that when you role model these descriptors and are passionate and positive, it sets off psychological responses in those around you. These are generated in your "mirror neurons." The mirror neurons are a key reason we have empathy and learn from role models.

In the article "Are We Wired for Empathy" by Six Seconds, we learn

Mirror neurons are "smart cells" in our brains that allow us to understand others' actions, intentions, and feelings. The mirror neurons are in many areas of our brains, and they fire when we perform an action such as grasping an apple, and similarly we see others doing it. As it turns out, our mirror neurons fire when we experience an emotion and similarly when we see others experiencing an emotion, such as happiness, fear, anger, or sadness. When we see someone being sad, for example, our mirror neurons fire and that allows us to experience the same sadness and to feel empathy. We don't need to "think" about the other person being sad, we actually experience it firsthand.[1]

Please remember, the research on mirror neurons is in its infancy, but is fascinating. Some doctors are postulating that dysfunction of mirror neurons is a possible cause of autism.[2] However, mirror neurons, and their existence, is a powerful explanation to why you can go to some classrooms and sense the positivity or negativity found in the room. The teacher sets the tone of the classroom and when you enter that room, your mirror neurons are replicating the tone set by the educator. This could possibly explain why you "feel" the positivity or the negativity in different settings of the same building. This is illustrated in the graphic found on page 33. Hopefully with time, the research into mirror neurons will be replicated and we can all learn from this.

When you are generating the "ultimate teacher descriptors" via nonverbal communication, you could possibly be firing off your student's mirror neurons. They are experiencing these powerful positive virtues firsthand. Over time this will inspire the students and generate intrinsic learning and behaving.

Six Seconds continues, "Through mirror neurons, emotions are contagious—so if we want to be more joyful (for example), a powerful action is to spend time with people who are full of joy."[3] This is powerful, the emotions and descriptors generated by our nonverbal communication is constantly firing the mirror neurons in our student's brains. This is the essence of how we are making them feel. When the students begin to describe you with the "ultimate teacher descriptors" the consequences for your classroom environment are enormous. As previously stated in this book, classroom observers can feel the positivity of classes where teachers are generating these feelings and attributes.

The article continues, "The power of mirror neurons is another compelling reason that leaders need to take responsibility for their own actions and choices. People are literally mirroring the leader's actions—and the leader's emotions. Simply showing up with more ideal behavior and an intentional emotional state is an important part of imparting these qualities to others. Since mirror neurons are "always on" leaders have a huge responsibility to monitor and manage themselves as role models."[4]

I have been told by my administrators, and I have heard from other administrators in different buildings, that when they are having a bad day, they would go do walk-throughs in rooms where they knew the teacher was positive. Being in these classrooms would energize them. The positivity was contagious. They would leave the room feeling different. The graphic on page 33 is an illustration of how this might possibly be happening.

Remember, much of the research on inspiration is based for the business world. How do companies and bosses inspire workers to be more productive? This knowledge and data are the same for educators. Replace leader with educator in the above quote and this takes on an educational realm. Educators are constantly being monitored by the students. You could say the students are more impressionable than adult employees, so this is even more important for an educator. Our kids are constantly observing us. Our actions are constantly making their mirror neurons fire. The kids are learning their behavior from our behavior. This, in its essence, is the key for classroom management and for inspiration.

You can see the importance of the ultimate teacher descriptors. When kids are describing who you are with these words, you are essentially teaching them how to reproduce these actions. These positive virtues then inspire them. When you inspire the kids to believe in who they are, a growth mindset is activated. The consequences are enormous for the kids.

Let's take a look at the "Ultimate Teacher Descriptors" in a new way.

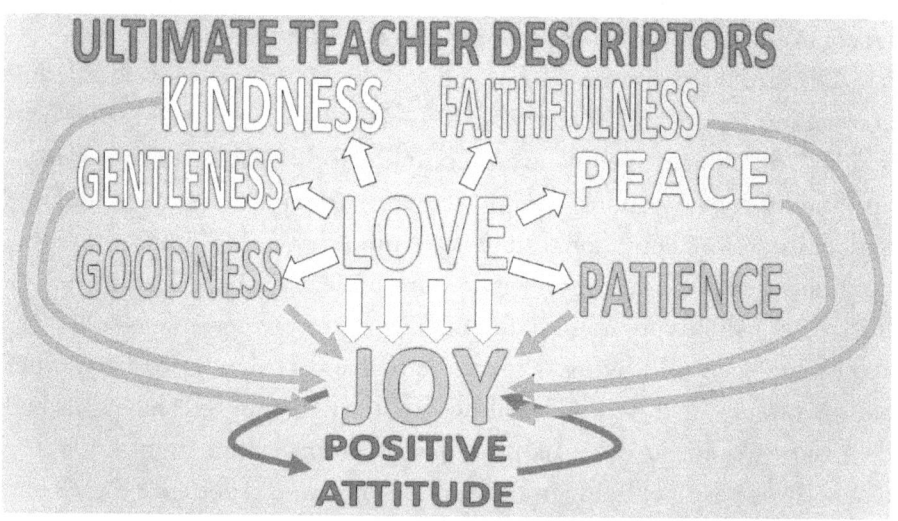

You are about to learn and to identify ways you can generate these descriptors. The actions described for doing this are based on the inspiration I have from making this my goal for three decades plus. The words found to reproduce these descriptors will be backed up by powerful student testimonials. Remember, there is no "inspire meter." You simply can't measure someone's ability to inspire. The research on this is fleeting and scarce. It is important you start writing down your thoughts when asked to do so. At the end of this book you will create a descriptor chart in which you will write down how you will reproduce each of these descriptors. No two humans are the same. We will generate these words in vastly different ways, but the outcomes on the students will be very similar.

Notice in this diagram LOVE is in the middle and the arrows all point away from love. Love for the students is the keystone for who you are as an educator. When you unconditionally love the students, and the students know they are loved just the way they are, the other descriptors will be easier to generate. Notice that all the arrows end up at JOY. This joy will change who you are. Joy is priceless. Joy will be the source of your inspiration to everyone around you. Joy will become a powerful force in a positive attitude cycle that will give your inspiration and non-verbal communication more power.

Inspired Phrase 935
The joy you receive from role modeling the ultimate teacher descriptors is the most powerful source of inspiration you can have over others to promote goodness.

The 935th inspired phrase that I wrote is a powerful truth in my life and it has the potential to be a truth in your life as well.

$\mathcal{L}$ove

～ઝઝૈ૦～

"Mr. Toups,

Thank you so much for helping me through the past two years. My grandpa died last year and without even realizing it, you helped me cope with the loss. I did not see a reason to live anymore, but you made me BELIEVE I could survive the depression and I did. I do not know if I would still be here if it weren't for you. You are a wonderful teacher, and you teach more than just math. Thank you sooo much! I will never forget you. You do not know this, but you have been like a father figure to me because my father is never around. I love you for that.

LOVE
—Charlotte"

Every teacher is told to "love" the kids, but no one really tells us how, largely because we are individuals and will do this in our own way. Verbal communicating your love will only get you so far. Love for your students is primarily generated through nonverbal communication. In the Ultimate Teacher Descriptor diagram on page 45, you can see that LOVE is at the heart of inspiration. When you properly love your students through nonverbal communication, the other descriptors can be generated.

Inspired Phrase 41
Love someone for who they are, and not what you would like them to be.

As educators it is imperative that we love our students JUST THE WAY THEY ARE! When a child walks in your room they need to know that they are loved and that they don't have to follow the rules to earn this. You need to teach the students correct behavior for all kids to learn, and there needs to be consequences for improper behavior, but your love should be unconditional.

Another powerful definition of love is often heard at many weddings. It was written by the apostle Paul in 1st Corinthians.

"⁴Love is patient and is kind, love does not envy, love does not parade itself, is not puffed up; ⁵does not behave rudely, does not seek its own, is not provoked, thinks no evil; ⁶does not rejoice in iniquity, but rejoices in truth; ⁷bears all things, believes all things, hopes all things, endures all things. ⁸Love never fails."

— *1ST CORINTHIANS 13 4-8 NJKV*

This definition of love is profound. When you can do these things with your students, your room will become a source of hope. The kids will want to be in your room. You will inspire them. Notice some of the most powerful things in this definition are "nots." Do not envy, do not parade your accomplishments in an arrogant way, do not be puffed up, do not be rude to the kids, and do not seek your own glory. Loving others means you are putting them ahead of you. This is huge. You probably will not survive long in education if you are making this job about "you." Once you realize as a teacher your life is about the kids you have been blessed to influence (it's not about you, but the kids), then your interactions with them will produce love and joy.

While doing Twitter chats, I created the LOVE diagram to show how I love my students through nonverbal communication. We will use this diagram as a reference on how we should love the students in our schools.

LOVE DIAGRAM

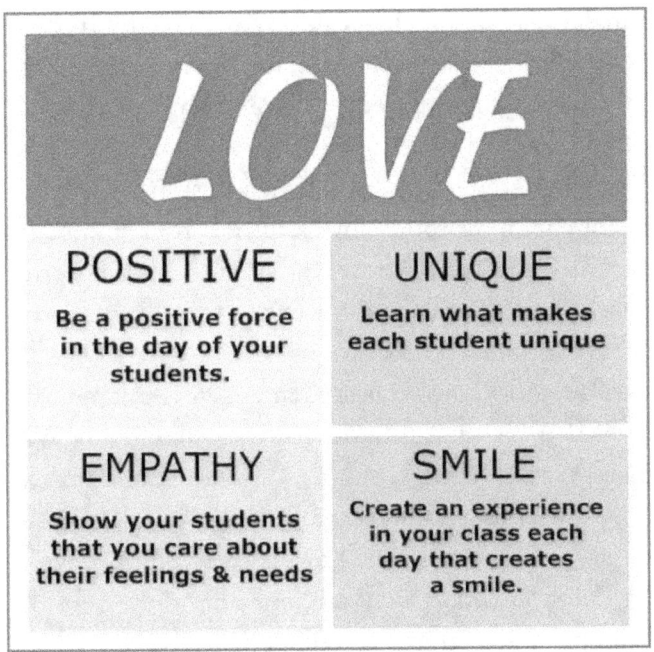

POSITIVE

The first step in my diagram to showing your students love is to be a positive force in the day of your students. Kids know which teachers are positive and not. When you are positive with the kids, they will want to be in your room. It will be a time of day they look forward to. When students are eager and anticipating your class period, the love that goes back and forth from the kids to the teachers will be generated.

Inspired Phrase 103
Those who are able to maintain a positive attitude at all times will soon become an inspiration to others.

It is overwhelming to me that I wrote this at the beginning of my teaching career. It is an absolute truth in my life and is verified through the research in mirror neurons.

Everyone can wake up and CHOOSE to be positive. This is a choice. When you make it a habit, your positivity will inspire those around you, and eventually this inspiration can turn into love. This love will become a powerful motivator. The difference of compelling others to act through fear of breaking a rule versus love is that the latter is the basis of your inspiration through the ultimate teacher descriptors. When kids are obedient in your room, through love and not through a set of rules you will develop intrinsically motivated students. This in turn will create students who behave, but also who want to learn. One powerful way to develop this love is to just be positive.

Secondly, do you know your students? Do you know each student? Do you know their favorite things, what they like to do? When the kids realize you are getting to know them as an individual, this will generate love. This love does not have a politically correct agenda. Love each individual kid that enters your room. Love is color blind. Love each kid for who they are. Tell each kid they are amazing; they were created to do wonderful things. They are all unique. TELL THEM THIS. Our kids, now more than ever, need to hear their lives will be impactful. Love is generated when you do this in a powerful way.

Third, be empathetic. The student letter that started this chapter is an excellent example of this. Your students need to know you care about them. This is done through nonverbal communication showing them that you have empathy for them. When you have a high school student that gets off a work shift at midnight and then SHOWS UP FOR SCHOOL the next day, the last thing they need to hear is their teacher griping at them for not doing their homework. The teacher should know the kid's situation, then thank them for being there. Show the students you care about them and do not complain to them. There is a fine line between complaining and encouraging them to be responsible. In the end you should be thankful the kid has made the effort to show up to your classroom. If you make the room positive and the students want to be in your room, they are likely to share this information with you. The kids will know you care about them. This can generate love.

Fourth, produce a smile. Make your classroom a place where kids want to be. Be a source of happiness each day in their life.

When you create a smile daily in the life of your student, they will look forward to coming to your room. Although this book stresses nonverbal communication, creating a smile is done largely through verbal communication. Say things that will create a smile. Changing your tone of voice can generate a smile. Develop a set of stories you share with your kids through the course of the year that will create a theme of happiness.

I started teaching in 1990. During the mid-90's I was watching *Home Improvement* and the antics of Tim Allen's Tim the Tool Man Taylor. I thought I could do this in my classroom. The kids absolutely love the grunts and the *More Power* chants. When I tell my "side stories" to the kids I just pretend I am Tim the Tool Man Taylor and I put on a show while making the kids smile.

The following is such an example.

"After finding the value that solves the equation, you can always check your answer by substituting the answer into the variable and show how both sides of the equation end up being the same. Hoo hoo hoo hoo hooo. (Tim Taylor grunt)"

This comes at the close of my lesson on how to solve multi-step equations using the antics of Tim Taylor. "Ashley, doesn't it feel kind of awesome that your answer actually makes the equation a true statement?" Ashley looks at me with a weird kind of face, while nodding her head like not really. The other students share similar faces. My students are now anticipating a "Toups Story" that will generate a smile.

I then ask a student who is not agreeing with me, "Brian, you don't get all happy and joyful when you solve an equation correctly?"

Brian replies, "Not really, Mr. Toups."

I then say, "Class, do you really want to know what it feels like when you start getting really hard math problems correct?" The class is eagerly awaiting the "Toups' Story." I continued to my junior high students, "Well, it is like this. Stephanie let us say you really, really like this boy, but no one else knows you like him. But he is so cute, and he is just such an amazing guy. Well, you go to an assembly in the gym and the principal is randomly sitting the students, so you don't sit by all your friends, and OMG you get to sit right next to the boy you have a crush on! Aah ho ho ho (Tim Taylor grunt). What do you say? Do you smile at him? What do you do? While you are trying to think of something to say to your heart throb you start getting all hot, your heart starts beating faster, your back starts getting sweat on it." I continue to go through a descriptive list of what "puppy love" does to you. The kids are all smiling. Then I close the story with, "Guys you know this feeling, right?" The kid's smiles are an affirmation that they have experienced this feeling of hormonal overload. Then I say with a huge smile, "This is what it will begin to feel like when you solve a math problem correctly. You will get all HOT. You will feel like that moment when you get to sit by the person you have a crush on. It will give you More Power!"

Stories like this are things your kids will remember. Later during the year when the thermostat is not working and the kids are saying, "Mr. Toups, why is it so hot in your room?" I will say, "Well, you are doing math, and when you do math it makes you feel so *hot*?" When it gets too cold in my room and the kids ask, "Mr. Toups, it's cold in here." In the world of modern schools where you really can't adjust the thermostat, I will reply with, "Well the administration knows this is a math class, and they know when you do math problems correctly it makes you feel so *hot*." I refer to this *"hot"* theme frequently during the year and the smiles that are produced are priceless. When kids associate you with a smile this in turn will develop into the kids saying you love them. This is another student testimony on how this story impacted them.

"Mr. Toups, I thank you sooo much for being an amazing math teacher. You have taught me so much and helped me out with my papers and grades. I think I would probably know nothing at all about math if it weren't for you. Every day when math is over you tell us to have an awesome day and it just makes things better. Also, it is soo funny when someone says it's hot and you say it's because we're thinking about math. Thanks for everything. Jessica"

Perhaps one of the most powerful things a student can say about their teacher is that they love them. This love is truly done nonverbally through a multitude of ways. Among these are being positive, knowing what makes a person unique, showing empathy to others, and just being the source of a daily smile. If you look at the ultimate teacher descriptor diagram, love will truly be the source of inspiring your students. The other descriptors will be generated when the kids know you love them. Love is at the epicenter of inspiration.

Inspired Phrase 809
When students know that their teacher loves them unconditionally, their fears and self-doubts will crumble. The students will begin to BELIEVE they can succeed.

Inspired Phrase 942
There is no limit to the size of your heart's ability to love others. Your ability to love magnitudes of people has no limits.

Inspired Phrase 66
The greatest gift you can give to another person is your love.

Inspired Phrase 41
Love someone for who they are, and not what you would like them to be.

Inspired Phrase 684
The end result of a teacher's love for their students is not only a child that is academically smarter in the content area, but also a child that is smarter in the lessons of life. The child is a more complete human being.

Inspired Phrase 847
Your power to change the lives of others all boils down to your unconditional love for them.

In my years as an educator there have been years when I have taught 200 plus students per day. Your heart is invigorated when you love your students. There is no limit to the amount of love you can shower on the kids who walk into your room every day. When the kids walk into your room and know they are loved, each day becomes a gift. Every teacher has the power to love every kid in every class. When you do this your job takes on a different dynamic. You will become a life changer. This is another example on how the power of love can connect people with vastly different backgrounds.

"Today I'm in tears. Happy tears...tears of joy. John's favorite teacher of all time and probably the one he will remember forever, came by our house today to give him a book he published about his own adversity and how he overcame it.

He chose 3 students from 9th grade that put their name in the raffle to receive this book. John didn't put his name in, but Mr. Toups came by and gave this to him anyway. He told John that he was one of his favorite students this year and that he reminded him of himself as a high schooler.

John would always come home telling me that this teacher was always lifting his spirits when others picked on him. Always telling him to "believe," always telling him that his success doesn't rely on how many friends he has or how popular he is. Such a positive force and attitude coming from someone who was always picked on as a child too. He would share his stories with John, and they have had a profound impact on him.

Today was a very emotional day for him, saying that when he is successful in life, he's going to come back to share his success with Mr. Toups. He said this was his happiest day in the past several months.

This is the impact that teachers can have on students when they notice them, when they notice their struggle. Seriously my heart is filled with gratitude towards this man that probably has very little in common with our family. But the love in his heart is what connected a proud Muslim boy to a proud conservative Christian teacher."

These journal entries will be used at the end of the book to make a personalized "ultimate teacher descriptor" chart. Please take time to fill these in so you can create your personalized chart at the end of the book.

PUT IT INTO ACTION

Who was someone outside of your family that you knew loved you?

What actions, other than words, made you realize this as a truth?

What are some actions you can do to illustrate you love your students?

Kindness

~∾∾⊃

The Collins Dictionary defines kindness as "the quality of being gentle, caring, and helpful."[1]

What say you? Write down what you think are the characteristics of a kind teacher.

I have often been described as being one of the most "kind teachers" a student will ever have. As illustrated in the "Ultimate Teacher Descriptor" diagram, your unconditional love for the students is at the heart of being kind. If the kids know they are loved for who they are when they are in your room, kindness is a powerful product of this love.

My definition of kindness is "actions showing the goodness of your heart regardless of what others do." This corresponds to "random acts of kindness." Being kind really is not generated by your words—it is your actions which are at the heart of random acts of kindness.

List down some examples of random acts of kindness that a teacher can do for a student.

This goes both ways, writing down random acts of kindness that students can do for each other, or for their teachers. List some of them here.

Some things on my list for teachers would be writing motivational words on a paper you are grading, acknowledging (by a tap on the shoulder, a nod of the head, a thumbs up, etc.) that your students are on task and doing what is desired, giving a student a sticker or motivational pick me up letter when you know they are going through a tough time, taking the time to email or call a parent with a positive message, or using social media to spread the positive things your students are doing.

Some things on my list for students would be sitting by someone at lunch, inviting a kid to play with them at recess, helping out a student with peer tutoring, giving other students who do something good a positive note, writing a thank-you letter to their teachers during Teacher Appreciation Week (you will read some of these letters I have received through my career in this book), and just helping other people when they see a need.

The single best way to teach kids how to be kind is to be a role model. When kids are aware their teachers are being kind in an unmerited way to them, they are more likely to do the same to their peers (remember, this is possibly done through mirror neurons). A school that encapsulates this in daily reminders and actions will take on a strong dynamic that will foster student learning and growth. The students will look forward to going to school.

One of my greatest acts of kindness is showing up to my students' after school events and getting *believe* selfies with them. Taking the time to edit the photos, then post them to social media is a powerful act of kindness. The kids are so happy when their selfie gets "Instagrammed" or better yet when their picture gets put on the #AlwaysBelieve" wall in my classroom. At the end of the year I cut out all the *believe* selfies and give them to the kids.

The *Always Believe* Wall

Another powerful act of kindness happens at the end of the year. My classroom is decorated with my inspired phrases that are made into posters with pictures I have taken. The students love reading the phrases as they come into my room. A student whom I did not teach was in my room for a benchmark test. She said, "How can you sit in this room and not be inspired? It's so positive here."

At the end of the year I have a drawing for the students who want to take home one of my posters. Actions like this are things your students will remember long after they leave your room. Legacies are generated when the kids have mementos from the year they were in your room.

PUT IT INTO ACTION

Write down some ways you have seen teachers create legacies through kind actions or ways that you would like to do this.

Who are your Mount Rushmore of people (either alive or dead) who were walking examples of kindness? Why did you pick each?

What are three ways a school-wide program can be developed to promote kindness?

Faithfulness

F aithfulness is defined by dictionary.com as being "strict or thorough in the performance of duty; true to one's word, promises, vows, etc.; steady in allegiance or affection; loyal; constant; reliable; trusted; believed; adhering or true to fact, a standard, or an original; accurate."[1] (https://www.dictionary.com/browse/faithful)

This definition gives a variety of examples of what it means to be "faithful." When you tell your students positive things, and your actions do not back your words, your students will consider you to be fake. When your actions and words are positively praising your work and your commitment to your students and school, this is being faithful.

My definition of faithful is "when your actions are true to your words." One of my coworkers once shared with me a tribute—a student was talking about me in the context of their class discussion and said "Mr. Toups is real. He loves you just the way you are. You do not have to earn love in his room. He is different." This was an LGBTQ student who saw the world as judging her for the choices she was making. She had absolute FAITH in me. Your unmerited and unconditional love for your students generates faithfulness. In a world of political correctness, teachers must be greater than the hate that is prevalent on social media and in our news. Love every student that sits in your room, PERIOD. When students know they are loved in your room for just being there, they will have faith in you.

~

"Mr. Toups,
I really want to thank you for all you have taught me the past two years. I am so grateful for your patience and faith that you have for each and every one of us. I know I can be a brat, but you always stay calm and never lose control. You have taught me many things, the main one being to always believe. In a world full of negativity, you always seem to find the bright side of every situation.
Thank you for being an awesome teacher!
Love Always, Kate"

Even if you think they are choosing wrong actions, you love them unconditionally. This letter illustrates how a student can view you as being faithful. Even though Kate knew her actions were not the best, she realized I would stay calm and collected. That just did not include her; that included everybody. When you treat students differently for the same behavior, the kids will lose their faith in you. Being consistent is a huge part of building faith with your students. Do your best not to have favorites. I often tell my students that they are all my favorite, and in a way, they know this to be true with me.

When students know you have faith in them, another powerful force is set into effect. If you make your first rule "Always Believe in Yourself," the kids can be inspired to acknowledge this as a truth for themselves. When your students know your faith in them exists, and that you believe in them, this creates a powerful dynamic in your room that is hard to match. The students will walk in your room with confidence. As previously mentioned by Tony Robbins, a growth mindset is learned when you start believing in your capabilities.[2] This growth mindset is critical in growing your students academically as well as socially. Eventually your faith in your students will inspire them to believe they can succeed. Since my career started in 1990, I have witnessed this happen over and over. When you can do this with 16-year-old eighth graders who have never been successful at school, you are changing lives. You are empowering a future of good in your students long after they leave your room.

Here are some more of my inspired phrases that relate to faith.

Inspired Phrase #839
As a teacher, when your students think of you when they are adults to get through tough times or make the right decision, you have taught them more than academics, you have influenced their life beyond words. This is the power of Always Believe in Yourself as your first rule.

Inspired Phrase #885
A teacher's inspiration in the classroom today has the potential to change the world for the better in the future.

Inspired Phrase #827 September
Nothing inspires people more than the testimony of your words and actions over an extended period of time.

PUT IT INTO ACTION

Who is someone outside of your family that you know had faith in you?

What actions, other than words, made you realize this as a truth?

What are some actions you can do to illustrate you have faith in your students?

Gentleness

~~~

"The teacher's gentleness was instrumental in effectively guiding her students in a unique way." What adjectives would you use to describe the teacher in the previous sentence?

Some definitions of gentleness are...
The quality or state of being gentle[1]
Gentle can be defined as
1. Considerate or kindly in disposition, amiable, tender
2. Not harsh or severe; mild and soft
3. Easily managed or handled; docile
4 refined and polite[2]
Dictionary.com also has a good definition:
Gentle, meek, mild refer to an absence of bad temper or belligerence.[3]

GENTLE has reference to disposition and behavior and often suggests deliberate or voluntary kindness or forbearance in dealing with others.

MEEK implies a submissive spirit and may indicate undue submission in the face of insult or injustice.

MILD suggests absence of harshness or severity, rather because of natural character or temperament than conscious choice.[3]

An article on Gentleness "Life, Hope, & Truth" says:

"What is gentleness? It is the humble and meek attitude of wanting to help other people instead of wanting to be superior to them. This attitude flows from a spirit of real love for the individual – having true, outgoing concern for their well-being. Such an attitude is shown in how we think about and treat others and what we say to them."[4]

Notice in this last definition, that the attitude of gentleness "flows from a spirit of real love for the individual." Your love for others will generate a gentleness in your actions.

Gentleness is also very closely related to empathy. Knowing how others are feeling and being gentle with them with this knowledge is a great example of gentleness. Your ability to share the stories of what you went through as a child is also a powerful source of gentleness. When the kids know you walked in their shoes, that you experienced similar tribulations and had the same feelings that they are having, a powerful connection is made. The relationship between the teacher and student goes up to another level.

In my book *The Story of Always Believe*, there is a story called "Blank Blank."

In fifth and sixth grade, I was the kid that everybody called names. I overcame this experience through ignoring most of it, but it was painful. The teacher that helped me overcome this was my PE Coach. His response to my situation in the story is an amazing example of gentleness.

Watch Mr. Toups read The Story of Always Believe - Blank Blank

Through this experience as a child, I have learned to not let negative actions affect me. As an adult, I am so slow to anger, including when my students do wrong. At times I have felt I should have reacted more profoundly to their misdeeds, but in retrospect, my gentleness probably overrides the harsh action involved through strict enforcement of classroom rules. Over time my student's actions are driven through their love for me. Their actions become intrinsic.

This method of classroom management is exceedingly difficult with middle school-aged boys. Many of the boys sense my "gentleness" as weakness and this guides their actions and misconducts, until they realize that my gentleness is generated through my love for them. Most of my years teaching middle school featured a very rough fall semester, but in the spring semester, the boys eventually came around. Sometimes the boy's hearts are too hardened, and I do not mold them in the year I teach them, but my actions eventually turn into seeds that come to bloom later in their life. One of the great moments of my career and a future "Mount Rushmore" moment found in this book is just such an example.

This note from an anonymous student is a powerful example of the power of gentleness and the ability to shape behavior with positive reinforcement.

"'Always Believe' is important to me personally because it shows me that I can and will do whatever I set my mind to. I see myself reflected in Mr. Toups and I see what he has become. When I look at how successful he is, I

cannot help but wonder what I can do when I get older! Thank you, Mr. Toups, for changing my life! I love you and your class!"

Inspired Phrase 680
Great teachers are able to motivate their students to succeed intrinsically.

Looking back on my career as a teacher since 1990, I passionately believe that my "gentleness" has been a great motivator for my students. The compassion role modeled to them is an essential lesson for them to learn empathy. When they see another adult besides their parents give them grace over improper actions over time this is a powerful lesson on guiding them to act correctly.

PUT IT INTO ACTION

Who was someone in your life that demonstrated gentleness?

What actions, other than words, made you realize this as a truth?

What are some actions you can do to illustrate gentleness to your students?

Goodness

~~~

Quite simply goodness means the absolute best.

Merriam Webster defines goodness as the quality or state of being good.[1]

Dictionary.com defines goodness as:

1 the state or quality of being good, moral excellence, virtue, kindly feeling; kindness; generosity...
4 excellence of quality
5 the best part of anything; essence; strength.[2]

When I think of goodness, I want the time the students spend in my room to be the absolute best minutes of their day.

Do your students *want* to be in your room, or do they *have* to be in your room?

As an educator, goodness is a characteristic of a human who is constantly putting the needs of the students first. They have unconditional love for ALL the kids, and they desire to be a blessing to their students. Referring to the flow chart of ultimate teacher descriptors, goodness is generated from loving your students. When the kids know you love them unconditionally, goodness can follow. You are probably not going to be described with the goodness adjective, but the kids might say your class is the best part of their day. You are very unlikely to be described with goodness without being described as kind, loving, generous, and virtuous. Goodness is generated through the love you have for others.

Goodness can be found in this student letter given to me in the spring of 2020.

"Goodbye, Mr. Toups, I had so much fun being one of your students this year. Not only did you help me really understand and succeed in Algebra, but you put a smile on my face and made me laugh every single day. I will never forget you and will most definitely come visit you next fall. Have a wonderful summer, Mr. Toups, and thank you for everything you have done. I will never stop believing."

The thing that sticks out to me in this student note is that I truly do try to do something each class period and every day that will generate a smile—whether it be one of my Tim the Tool Man Taylor grunts, funny face, or just saying something funny. If the kids know they will come to your room and get a smile each and every day, your class will be a source of goodness in their life.

On a humorous note, something I do in my room to illustrate goodness (the absolute best of anything) is to compare the math problems in my room to happiness and fun. "Students, do you know where else you can see this problem about linear systems?" They all shake their heads no. "Do a Google image search for fun and BAM! This problem will pop up." The kids will just shake their heads; some may even say, "Mr. Toups, I don't think so."

After completing a multistep problem, I will often compare the feeling of getting the answer right to goodness by using one of my favorite foods, the Oreo cookie.

Watch Mr. Toups tell his students how to correctly eat an Oreo cookie

There are many other things that you can compare to goodness—the center of a Cinnabon (a Cinnabon tenderloin). The icing on a cake. The evening that the sun kisses the clouds producing a brilliant red, orange, yellow, and blue sunset sky.

The great moments in your life and the magical moments of your childhood and other stages of your life are goodness. Do something each day in your room to try to make a moment that will be the "goodness" of your student's day. Remember this letter and how this is a testimony to this.

"Mr. Toups,
You are by far the best teacher I have ever had in my entire life. Every day I look forward to coming to your class.
ALWAYS BELIEVE – John"

PUT IT INTO ACTION

Look back at your time as a student. What educator stands out on creating goodness moments in their class period?

What educator had a class that was the best part of their day?

What did they do to make those moments?

What are your "Mount Rushmore" goodness events of your life? These events are the moments you remember when you feel blue or when times are tough. Who was responsible for these moments?

What are some actions you can do to produce goodness moments in your classroom?

$\mathcal{P}atience$

~~~

T he Free Dictionary gives the following examples of being patient:

1 Bearing or enduring pain, difficulty, provocation, or annoyance with calmness
2 Tolerant understanding
3 Capable of calmly awaiting an outcome or result; not hasty or impulsive[2]

Remember, patience in a teacher can take on a different dynamic. A teacher's power with patience is exhibited when they do not let the kids "get to them." The teacher restrains their anger and somehow uses LOVE to generate a desirable outcome.

Patience is perhaps the descriptor produced from LOVE that brings out the superhero in a teacher. In many classrooms the behavior of students is generated from fear of being disciplined for breaking a rule. However, if a student in your room knows they won't get snapped at for a simple misconduct and that their behavior will be redirected with love, then their behavior in your room can change from that of fear of being disciplined for rule breaking to acting out in love for the common good of the learning environment. This is not easy to accomplish. Kids need to learn that when their behavior stops other kids from learning, it is not acceptable. The key is how you respond to these actions. Will the behavior in your room be generated from rule-following, or will it the kids intrinsically behave because of the patience generated from your love to each student? If the students sense you only love them because of their obedience to rules, creating intrinsically behaved kids will be tough.

Patience is also vital for middle school and junior high teachers. Kids between 13 and 15 are impacted by the hormones of adolescence. According to Warren & Brooks-Gunn:

> "The hormonal stages revealed a significant curvilinear trend for depressive affect, impulse control, and psychopathology scales, indicating significant changes in these behaviors during times of rapid increases in hormone levels. These data suggest that hormonal changes may be more important than the physical changes as determinants of certain mood and behavior patterns at adolescence."[3]

They have trouble thinking of others. Their thoughts are often centered around "me." At moments, you will be teaching how they should behave in a collaborative classroom. Rules are needed in these moments, but try your best to redirect behavior with your love through patience, rather than automatically enforcing rule-breaking consequences.

SELF-CARE AND PATIENCE

A teacher's self-care is immensely intertwined with patience. As an educator, you should be making your life about the kids you are blessed to impact. This happens day after day. If you are failing to do things to release the tension produced every day, you will eventually snap. Self-care is vitally important to your success as an educator. Make sure you are getting down time. Do things you enjoy. Exercise is a great release.

During my years teaching in a rural school district, I had property that backed up to the woods. There were many days after school in which I came home, got an ax, went to the woods, and swung away at my frustrations.

Remember, you are working with kids, not robots. The kids will have bad days as well. They will have days where they vent in your room. Your ability to display patience during these times is huge. Other students will notice how you respond to misbehavior. If they figure out that they can work together to get you to snap, beware. Junior high kids can be tough. I have had years where the kids have driven away more than one teacher from the profession. If you are not releasing the frustrations, you might be building up with the patience you are having with your kids, you are likely to experience teacher burn out.

PUT IT INTO ACTION

Write the Mount Rushmore of adults in your life (past and present) that are role models of patience.

Write down the Mount Rushmore of your "stress relief" activities. Make sure you are finding the time during the year to do these activities.

Write out your definition of teacher patience. What are actions you can do to demonstrate your patience?

P_{eace}

~~ mark ~~

P eace can have many definitions. Search for a definition for peace, and you may get the following results:

The absence of war; freedom from internal commotion; freedom from private quarrels; freedom from agitation or disturbance by the passions, as from fear, terror, anger, anxiety or the like; quietness of mind; tranquility; calmness; quiet of conscience.[1]

In terms of being an educator and what peace means in a classroom, this definition is what I would like to use: "freedom from disturbance, tranquility." Another way you can think of peace is that you turn your classroom into a safe place for your students. Your classroom will become a place your kids want to be in. It is a place where the kids know they are loved. An educator's unconditional love for all their students will generate a "peaceful" classroom.

If an educator excels at this, the peace in their classroom can be felt as you walk into the room. Principals and other educators who do walk-throughs or observe classrooms know what I am talking about here. Some classrooms have a "vibe" that feels "peaceful." There is order and love present as you stand in the room. Great educators can generate this vibe. Merriam-webster.com defines vibe as a distinctive feeling or quality capable of being sensed.[2] A bing.com search for vibe definition gives this, a person's emotional state or the atmosphere of a place as communicated to and felt by others.[3] Collinsdictionay.com defines vibe as the good or bad atmosphere that you sense with a person or place.[4] Remember the mirror neurons are also possibly involved in this. Your students will possibly be replicating your actions when their mirror neurons are activated. I wish all educators could experience the feeling generated by a classroom that has peace.

I have been told more than once from college students observing classrooms that my classroom "feels different." They did not know how to express this feeling in words, but it is the "peace" of my room that is generated through the love I have for my students.

If you look at the collinsdictionary.com definition again, this "vibe" can also be a bad atmosphere. I have been in classrooms where this "bad atmosphere" is present. The teacher has generated a classroom of negativity. The students are allowed to behave in a selfish manner. The classroom is not about "we," it is about "me." When you walk in a room like this, you will sense the opposite of tranquility. You will sense friction. The class feels like it is about to erupt. Again, principals and educators involved in walk throughs and teacher observations know this feeling.

Just like a classroom that has "peace," the classroom with the bad atmosphere is also generated by the teacher. In most instances, this bad atmosphere is generated through the teacher's negativity. The teacher can be negative about several things. When this is orally and non-verbally communicated to the students, the student's behavior will likely alter to negativity and will be empowered by the negativity of the teacher. A student that is a behavior problem in a class that has a negative atmosphere may likely be the best-behaved student in a classroom that has "peace."

There have been parent conferences I have attended in which the student is poorly behaved in all their classrooms, except for mine. Again, principals reading this can think of meetings like this. How does this one teacher generate good behavior from a kid who is consistently written up for bad behavior in all the other classrooms? The educators that can do this are using (whether they know it or not) the nonverbal communication skills being taught in this book. They are non-verbally communicating unconditional love to all their kids, and this in turn is generating the other ultimate teacher descriptors of kindness, gentleness, goodness, faithfulness, patience, and "peace."

When kids know they are loved as who they are, they are likely to behave correctly out of love generated by the educator. The class will be the "goodness" in their day. They are likely to be kind to their peers. They know their teacher has faith in them and is patient with them.

Speaking of faith. In the book of James 1:3 it says, "the testing of your faith produces patience." What a profound thought as an educator. Over the years you will have various students that truly will test your faith. Over the course of a career that lasts decades an educator will become more patient with all kinds of students. This is very likely produced by the educator developing and having faith in their kids.

A career in education hinges on the ability to make your students successful. A huge component of this success is the teaching having faith in each and every kid. This faith, over time, results in the teacher developing patience with kids which results in a classroom that prevails with peace.

Students are unlikely to describe who you are with "peace," but they know that your classroom is a safe zone for them each day. This drawing is a testimony to the peace being written about in this chapter.

This was given to me one January day by a student. Notice the words found on this poster. This is what the student is using to describe me. The student, without a doubt, is conveying I believe in them. Also notice that love and peace both appear. Just looking at the words on this poster illustrates the power of the words in this book. This child is unlikely to forget the moments in my classroom. Although the goal of my daily class time is the academic content, the true goal is for the students to view who I am with love, joy, peace, patience, goodness, gentleness, and kindness. When an educator achieves this, the academic content will follow. The learning and behavior will become intrinsic. Your classroom will take on a dynamic that can literally be felt. The kids will look forward to coming to your class. This all starts through the unconditional love you have and show to each individual child.

PUT IT INTO ACTION

Name the Mount Rushmore of adults you knew in your life, either as a child or as an adult, that generated the "vibe" of peace.

How did these adults generate their "vibe" of peace?

Do you believe you generate the "vibe" of peace? If not, what are steps you can take so this happens?

If you are an administrator or an educator involved in observing teachers, write down your Mount Rushmore of educators who have the "vibe" of peace that is present in their classes. If you are a teacher, write down coworkers you know that generate the "vibe" of peace?

How can you empower other educators to generate the "vibe" of peace in their classes?

Joy

I f you notice on the diagram of Ultimate Teacher Descriptors, JOY is the product—or it is generated when others around you describe who you are with these descriptors? What is JOY? Is joy the same as happiness?

Merriam Webster defines joy as:
1 The emotion evoked by well-being, success, or good fortune or by the prospect of possession of what one desires.
2 a state of happiness or felicity.
3 a source or cause of delight.[1]

Dictionary.com defines joy as:
1 the emotion of great delight or happiness caused by something exceptionally good or satisfying; keen pleasure; elation.
2 a source of keen pleasure or delight; something greatly valued or appreciated.
3 the expression or display of glad feeling, festive gaiety.
4 a state of happiness or felicity.[2]

Before I begin my testimony of how my career as an educator has been a joy generator, I would like to say that joy is not the same as happiness. A toddler opening presents on Christmas morning may display joy in getting the gifts. The gifts that the toddler desired generated happiness which might be displayed as joy, but after a few weeks the happiness generated by the gifts will subside. Material items and the pursuit of them generates happiness. Just as the gifts at Christmas, the happiness will subside, and the pursuit of a new material item will take over. When you base your life on the pursuit of material items, the happiness that you seek will only be momentary. The pursuit of material items will only lead to a void and meaningless life that has flashes of happy times that eventually slip into pursuit of the next and greatest item.

The following sentences are some of my inspired phrases that are truths in my life concerning happiness and joy.

Happiness based on material things will be fleeting. Happiness based on making others become better is everlasting, and will turn into joy.

The pursuit of material wealth to produce happiness will lead to an empty and void life. The pursuit of giving your life away to make others become better will feel your soul with priceless joy.

When you make your life about ME the pursuit of external currency will never be quenched. Contentment will never come upon you. When you make your life about others, in the currency of JOY you will be rich. Contentment will rule your thoughts. Your life will have meaning through loving others.

No matter what your occupation is, you are always in a position to serve others and make them shine bright. If you do this your livelihood will become a source of joy that will fill your heart and make your monetary paycheck insignificant.

Life in the pursuit of things results in the accumulation of stuff, life spent in the pursuit of loving others results in a meaningful life that produces priceless joy.

Others will tell you over and over that life is about making others become better. When this becomes reality, your life will be filled with joy.

Every day you have the power to make someone have a better day. When you do this, joy will fill your soul.

Teachers that produce joy in their relationships with their students will inspire them beyond the walls of their school.

Money can provide temporary happiness, but if your foundation for happiness is on material items, it will be fleeting. When your foundation for happiness comes from serving others, this happiness will turn into joy which is permanent and everlasting.

Your job as an educator "should" center around making those around you (not just your students, but also your co-workers) better. When the above sentences become reality in your life, your job as an educator will morph into a joy generator.

Students will say, "Mr. Toups, why are you happy every day?"

"Mr. Toups, do you ever get sad?"

These are questions posed by my students in the spring. Day after day, they come to my room and are a part of the joy that my job generates. Joy, unlike happiness, will never subside. The primary way an educator can have a job that generates joy is to turn their life into a life of service and always put the kids' lives ahead of their own. When you make others shine bright, the joy that overcomes your soul will make your actions and words become a shining beacon of hope to others. As you continue to inspire others by using the ultimate teacher descriptors, the joy that is generated will continue to cycle and be regenerated. This is an immensely powerful process. If this cycle ever becomes a truth in your life, you will wake up and want to go to work. A conversation with my coworkers and administrators throughout my career will confirm this.

The following sentences are powerful forces when educators realize them. The sentences italicized in the rest of this section are also some of my inspired phrases that have become reality in my career.

When your passions turn into making others better, joy will fill your heart and contentment will rule over your desires.

When you spread love, joy, and kindness to others, your life will become a shining beacon of hope to those around you.

When teachers love their students for who they are, joy will fill their heart and contentment will rule their actions. They will be able to overlook student misbehavior as foolish actions and guide them to proper actions.

When you realize that as a teacher your life is about the kids you have been blessed to influence, that it's not about you but kids, then your interactions with the kids will produce joy.

The last sentence holds powerful truths. Find a teacher that is burning out, or who is a constant complainer. They are making their jobs more about them than they are the kids. As an educator it is hard to persevere year after year if you are not going to work to be with the kids. Joy will leave your presence when your daily goals turn into ME.

Another powerful way to produce joy is to share your story with your students and coworkers. I have talked about my story through this book and the importance of sharing these is being reemphasized. When others know that you went through trials they are going through, your relationship with them will take on a different dynamic. As a youth, I had an eye injury at five-years-old that forever changed the direction of my life.

When I was in fifth and sixth grade, I was the kid that everyone picked on when I was at school. The summer before my ninth-grade year, I was at home when my father attempted suicide. These powerful stories I share with my students create a connection I have with them that perseveres long after they leave my room. Joy is produced when you help others go through a tribulation that you persevered in your past.

Perhaps the most powerful force of joy generated is that when you know deep in your heart that when you wake up and go to work you are fulfilling your "it." When you know your purpose and you know that without a doubt your job is providing you a means of fulfilling your purpose, the joy that is generated from this permeates your very being. When you use your talents to improve the lives of others, joy will fill your soul. There is no limit to the amount of joy that your body can hold. One of my coworkers at summer camp once said, "TEX (my alias at my summer camp), you have found your *it*. There are lots of people who live their whole lives and never find it." One of my Mount Rushmore days of my career involves me finding the "it" of my life.

If you don't know your "why," or your "it," I would strongly suggest reading Barbara Bray's book *Define Your Why*. This book will guide you using amazing activities that will help you figure out why you are here and what your "it" actually is.

My summers at my summer camp were also a dynamic way that joy was generated in my life. The summer of 1989 was the most magical summer of my life. I was the general cabin counselor to a group of six ten-year-old boys. I still remember their names like yesterday. These six boys changed my life. It was here I discovered my talents to inspire and create happy moments with children. I spent all day every day with these kids, and we even slept in the same cabin. We became like a family. The memories we made in the summer of 1989 still produce joy in my life.

In 2001, the fifth summer I spent at my summer camp, I became the first full-time camp photographer. For 14 summers, I took thousands upon thousands of pictures of the greatest moments of a kid's life. This profoundly changed me and had a huge impact on my role as an educator. Each day I was part of a kid's greatest memory. My ability to inspire the counselors to create these magical memories also helped me develop my talents as an educator.

The summers I spent at this camp led to this truth in my life:

The joy you receive when you become part of a child's happiest memories is truly worth more than any monetary paycheck.

Through the moments I have seen as a camp photographer, I firmly believe that when you produce a happy memory, that lasts a lifetime with a child who is in the innocence of their childhood; the joy that is generated from this is perhaps the most powerful of all. Think back to the innocence of your childhood when you were at the age when you believed in the magic of Santa, or when you believed your dad was as powerful as Superman. Maybe you believed your mother's love can heal even the worst wounds. The happy memories you have with the adults of this time are truly life-touching. They are perhaps the golden coins in the treasure chest of happy memories. If you are a teacher of fourth graders who are younger, you wake up every day with the potential to create one of these memories. All educators wake up each day with the potential to do this. Treasure each moment with every student that is in your room. Do your best to make memories that the kids will remember. The lessons your kids will remember about you are not the academic lessons; they are the lessons of what it truly means to be a genuine and loving human being. These lessons are generated by the very topic of this book. The nonverbal communication skills that generate these memories will in essence generate the moments that will be remembered long after the kids leave your presence.

The picture to the right is one of the all-time greatest pictures I have taken of joy being generated. Notice that the smiles on both people show the magic of the moment. This little boy might actually believe that he is flying. The young man who is generating this memory is also being blessed with joy. What even brings more greatness to this picture is that the counselor in this picture is my son. Seeing my child generate a magical moment like this is amazing as a parent. As the camp photographer, every day I saw moments like this. Young counselors, many of them aspiring to a career in education, making memories with the campers. The happy memories that persevered after camp was over actually generate joy that lasts long after the summer. They truly last a lifetime and so does the joy.

Loving others not only generates the other ultimate teacher descriptors, it is a powerful way to generate joy. I passionately believe this is a fundamental truth of life.

Your level of joy is dependent on how much you love others.

I use this phrase as part of my introduction to functions and replace dependent with "function of." The more you love others, the joy that permeates your being is increased. There is no limit to the joy that can be filled in your being. If your body is a five-gallon container, it can be filled with ten gallons of joy as you love others. Joy is not dependent on your relationships with others, it is dependent on your free will to love others, regardless of what they think of you. I also believe the greatness of a teacher depends on their ability to love any kid.

When you realize that your body is an instrument to show love for humanity, joy will fill your soul.

This is a powerful thought of realizing your body is a mere instrument to show love to others.

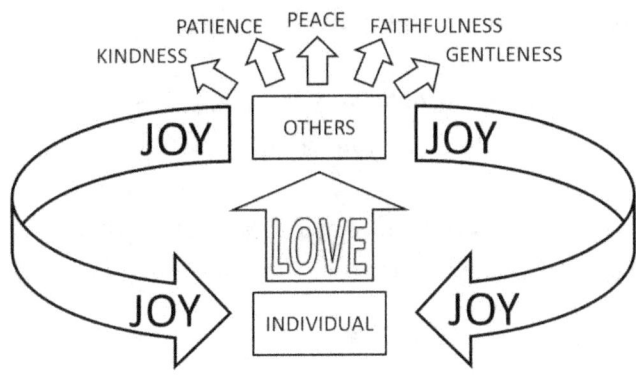

The joy you receive from role modeling the ultimate teacher descriptors is the most powerful source of inspiration you can have over others to promote goodness.

This joy can be felt by your mere presence. When you begin to live the topics of this book and your job begins to generate joy, your room will "feel" different. There will be a positive aura that can be felt not just by your students but also to those who come in.

Perhaps the greatest component of the joy that is generated from role modeling the ultimate teacher descriptors is the force of inspiration that you will have over your kids. Your kids will remember the positive messages you give. When I started teaching in 1990 and I made my first rule "Always Believe in Yourself," and later that year, I also made it my goal for my kids to describe me with love, joy, kindness, gentleness, goodness, faithfulness, peace, and patience. I really didn't realize the powerful force of these two combined. Like my mentor, the teacher told me, "You can't make the kids believe without a consequence; it is probably not a good classroom rule." You cannot make them believe but you can inspire them. When you inspire a child to believe they can be successful, you impact them beyond comprehension. You literally change their lives.

When you inspire others to believe they can succeed, indescribable joy will fill your heart.

As an educator having your being filled with joy is a result of living a life that role models the ultimate teacher descriptors. When you do this with the kids in your community, this joy is magnified exponentially.

I would like to finish this topic of joy with the inspired phrases (many of them were used in this chapter) that talk about joy.

When you empower others to believe they can succeed, joy will overcome your soul.

Happiness based on material things will be fleeting, happiness based on making others become better is everlasting and will turn into joy.

Joy that never ends results when you are cognizant of your purpose and that you are giving your life to make others shine bright.

The joy that fills your heart when you make others shine bright, will turn your mere presence into a lighthouse of hope for those you encounter.

The joy you receive when you become part of a child's happiest memories is truly worth more than any monetary paycheck.

Your level of joy is dependent on how much you love others.

When teachers love their students for who they are, joy will fill their heart and contentment will rule their actions. They will be able to overlook student misbehavior as foolish actions and guide them to proper actions.

The pursuit of material wealth to produce happiness will lead to an empty and void life. The pursuit of giving your life away to make others become better will feel your soul with priceless joy.

When you inspire others to believe they can succeed, indescribable joy will fill your heart.

When you walk the talk with others this is good, when you walk the talk with kids, and through your actions, kids are steered to what is right, priceless joy will fill your soul, your influence will live on through those kids.

Every day you have the power to make someone have a better day. When you do this, joy will fill your soul.

Teachers that produce joy in their relationships with their students will inspire them beyond the walls of their school.

∾

PUT IT INTO ACTION

Go back through this chapter and circle your Mount Rushmore (top four) ways that Joy is generated in someone's life.

Positivity/Joy Cycle

B eing positive will inspire others. When you inspire others, you will make them shine. When you make others shine your heart is filled with joy. When your heart is filled with joy, you will have a positive attitude. Your positive attitude will inspire others. The cycle will continue and intensify. It all starts by CHOOSING to be positive.

This phrase is a powerful truth in my life.

This is also true in my life:

Those who are able to maintain positive attitudes at all times will soon become a source of inspiration to others.

I wrote this phrase during my last year in college, not realizing the true impact of this in my future career as an educator. Being positive is a choice each person makes every day when they wake up. As an educator, your choice to be positive with your students and your coworkers will have perhaps the greatest impact on your career. Your ability to inspire those around you largely rests on your ability to remain and be a constant source of positivity.

I would like to add here that in "normal" life you are likely to have cycles of feelings that include both positivity and negativity. Grief due to tragic consequences is a "normal" part of life. However, when this positivity / joy cycle is prevalent in your life, your stages of grief due to tragedy could have different dimensions. For instance, at a funeral you might be more likely to focus on the good memories you have made instead of constantly focusing on the loss that has happened in your life.

The "spot" mentioned at the beginning of this book is a powerful force in my life. I often go to the picnic table pictured at the beginning of the book when my life is taking on more negativity and grief. While I am at this spot, my life becomes focused again. I often leave with a sense of guidance and reasoning as to the grief and the downward spiral of my current situation. Your ability to overcome and go through stages of grief is a huge part of becoming a functional adult, and as an educator, role modeling how you deal with tough times that are school related is just as important as role modeling the ultimate teacher descriptors.

I was blessed to have a co-worker as my next-door neighbor who was a former minister. We had so many talks about the topics found in this book. He noticed my daily positivity and knew it was generated from the joy that my job was producing in my life. I asked him if it was natural to be positive during times of tribulation (which I have been). His response was that the joy found within you can still naturally be present in times of trauma. Your mindset is different. Instead of thinking of the negativities of the situation, your mindset will think of the joyful memories you have made before the time of trauma. The conversations I have had with him have stayed with me and have confirmed the daily constant positivity that exists in my life.

Those that are constant beacons of positivity can also drown out negativity. This was written by one of my former coworkers.

"Jerry Toups, I remember sitting waiting for a meeting to start where everyone was griping, then you walked in the room, and everyone instantly changed their tune. So, I asked why. One person said, 'Toups can't stand complaining.' Someone else added, 'Plus, his positivity is fragile. We must protect it.' I was fascinated by that exchange. I thought a lot about it. That conversation is what motivated me to let everyone know I was on a quest to be positive, and it was a fragile situation so pipe down the negative."

Through this testimony you can see the impact of what a constant positive force can have not just on your students, but also the coworkers. When a teacher is constantly positive the kids will realize this. Your classroom will become a positive force in their daily life. It will be the "goodness" of their day.

If you look at the diagram of the ultimate teacher descriptors on page 43, you will see that positive is at the bottom of the diagram, and it forms a cycle with joy. When writing my first book, *The Story of Always Believe*, I had to write in words what the power of being positive meant in my life. I have been described by many of my coworkers and students as the most positive person they have ever known.

Your choice to be a constant source of positivity is also a huge source of your personal "vibe." People who do not know you will sense your positivity without saying a word. The same is for the opposite of positivity. If you continue to be a source of negativity, you will generate a negative vibe. This will generate likewise behavior. Students have often said to me, "Mr. Toups, you just make people smile." When I am riding my bike or walking in my neighborhood, I will constantly tell the people I pass by to "have an awesome day." The result is a smile. While riding my bike, I can point to those who pass me by in the other direction and they will almost always smile in return. Each time this happens, joy is being generated and strengthened in my very being.

The cycle of positivity/joy in my life is profound. More than once people who know me see me with my wife, they will ask, "Is he always positive? Does he ever have a bad day? Is he always like while he is at work?"

My wife once replied, "When I married him, it was like getting a puppy that never grows up. He is always so positive and happy."

Why is my positivity so profound? Since 1990, I have been striving to be a role model of the ultimate teacher descriptors. The descriptors, love, gentleness, goodness, patience, peace, joy, kindness, and positivity, have become a way of life for me. My job truly generates joy in my life. The amount of joy that can fill your being is unlimited. Just choosing to be positive each day will inspire your students. It is a powerful practice to do each day.

Rob Greenfield has stated, "In my experience people are turned off pretty quickly by anger, negativity and doom and gloom. People want to have a good time. I recommend being excited about what you are sharing and trying to be positive."[1]

Another article by E. Sterling states, "Staying positive is inspirational. This is a huge part of being inspirational. There have been times in my life where I've gotten depressed about a situation. A coach, friend, or family member has come by and boosted my morale just by being positive."[2]

In the spring of my first year of teaching, I was asked by my principal to teach a class to my coworkers on how to be positive. This was my very first time teaching a professional development class, and it was in the first year of my career. I was in a temporary building outside of the school and the principal saw the impact I was having with my positivity. This happened in the spring of 1991. Decades later, this positivity has only grown and strengthened in my life. My positivity is a driving force into my ability to inspire my students to *Always Believe*. It all starts each morning when I wake up and choose to have a positive day.

Here is another one of my inspired phrases that talks about positivity:

People with positive attitudes realize they are a PRODUCT of their past and not a circumstance of their past. They realize their trials molded and forged them into a better person. People with negative attitudes hold grudges on the negatives of their past. These grudges rot their inner core and make contentment impossible.

PUT IT INTO ACTION

In your life, either as an adult or a child, write down your Mount Rushmore of positive people. They can be friends, or adults in your life.

What was the source of their positivity?

How did you "feel" when you were around them?

What are the impacts of making your classroom a positive beacon in the lives of your students?

Maslow's Hierarchy of Needs

W hile writing this book, it has become apparent that the non-verbal communication skills mentioned and the ability to inspire others to *Always Believe* correspond to Maslow's Hierarchy of Needs, as well as to SEL (Social and Emotional Learning). Let us look first at Maslow's Hierarchy of Needs.

In 1943 Abraham Maslow published "A Theory of Human Motivation." The theory suggests that the most basic of human needs must be met and then individuals can go up to the higher levels of needs often illustrated in a pyramid.[1]

This is a diagram I made of Maslow's Hierarchy of Needs.

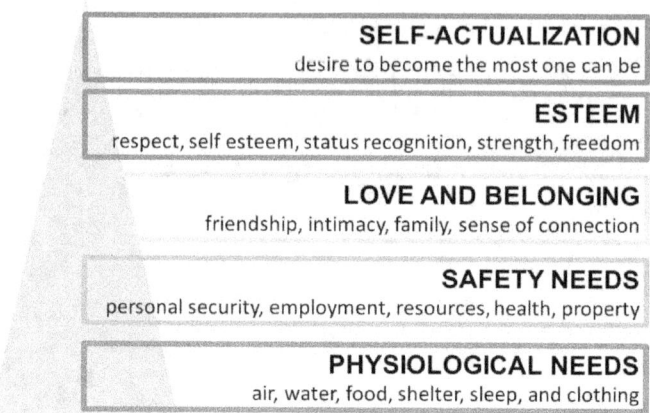

MASLOW'S HIERARCHY OF NEEDS

SELF-ACTUALIZATION
desire to become the most one can be

ESTEEM
respect, self esteem, status recognition, strength, freedom

LOVE AND BELONGING
friendship, intimacy, family, sense of connection

SAFETY NEEDS
personal security, employment, resources, health, property

PHYSIOLOGICAL NEEDS
air, water, food, shelter, sleep, and clothing

According to Simple Psychology, only two percent of the population ever get to the self-actualization portion of this diagram.[2] Thankfully in my career I have been blessed where most of the kids I teach come to school with the physiological and safety needs met. Through my experiences with nonverbally communicating the ultimate teacher descriptors, when a child is inspired to *Always Believe,* they climb up this hierarchy diagram and as adults, they remember this inspiration and can possibly approach the self-actualization level.

The physiological needs level of this hierarchy hopefully are obtained before the kids come to school. Schools in situations where these needs are not met face tremendous obstacles. Kids will have a tough time learning when they are wondering if they will get to eat supper that night, or where they will sleep.

In the article *Maslow's Hierarchy of Needs in Education,* McLeod states, "One human psychologist suggests that this occurs because immediate needs determine the immediate action of the student. When they are worried about these things, they focus solely on those distractions.

Those preoccupations will take priority over education and accomplishment."[2]

The author continues to talk about the physiological needs and how if clothing, food, hygiene, and sleep are not being provided that students will be unable to prioritize learning.[3]

There are extraordinary challenges when teaching students who do not have all their physiological needs met at home. Through my experiences, the love you have for these kids does make a difference. Do your best to make the kids know they are loved.

Safety needs in a classroom refer to a safe place generated by the teacher. The kids know they will be respected and loved. The classroom behavior management generated by the teacher exists and is enabling the students to learn in an environment that they know is secure. "Teachers should foster an environment that allows for healthy levels of risk-taking, question asking and answering, open thought sharing, and healthy discussion. They should not feel fearful of judgment from other students. Students crave a trust-based relationship with their teacher," shares McLeod.[4]

When your classroom behavior management reaches a level to where the kids are behaving intrinsically through the love they have for you, the LOVE AND BELONGING level of this diagram could be reached. The love and belonging level features a class where students demonstrate that there is friendship, trust and acceptance, receiving and giving affection of love, and they are part of the group.

McLeod continues: "As teachers and leaders, it is important to regard each student as a unique individual, appreciating them for their one-of-a-kind character traits. Emphasize healthy, positive behavior and self-esteem. Make an effort to show students that their hard work and dedication are genuinely appreciated."[5]

This level can be generated through the nonverbal communication of the ultimate teacher descriptors. This does not just happen in the first few days of the school year. The time needed to establish a classroom where behavior is managed through love may take well into the spring, depending on the social and emotional level of the kids in your class. If you are a secondary teacher, you may have class periods that reach this level in the fall, and yet other classes may not reach this until after the winter holiday break.

Once the classroom becomes a haven of "peace," the esteem-level can possibly be reached. This classroom will generate a positive vibe and feel different. The kids behave and learn through the love generated in this room. This is a room that the kids want to be in. Characteristics of the esteem level include students who have achieved dignity, mastery, and independence. They know they can achieve academic goals. Not only can they be successful at the academic goals they can also teach their peers. If you are not giving the kids time in your room so they can teach and learn from others, this level may not be achieved. I cannot tell you how many times I have had students tell me, "Mr. Toups, I have never been good at math until I had you as a teacher." When kids begin to feel this way, they could possibly be at the esteem level of Maslow's Hierarchy.

According to McLeod, "As teachers and leaders, it is important to regard each student as a unique individual, appreciating them for their one-of-a-kind character traits. Emphasize healthy, positive behavior and self-esteem. Make an effort to show students that their hard work and dedication are genuinely appreciated."[6]

The self-actualization level is individual. In my opinion, children that never come to a point where they believe they can succeed will not obtain self-actualization. The keystone to your very being is believing in yourself. As an educator, when you become part of inspiring a child to *Always Believe,* you are teaching at a level that goes way beyond the academia goals of your job. You are teaching kids to become better human beings on their possible pathway to self-actualization. You are inspiring the kids through your love to find their "IT," their purpose in life. One of the greatest accomplishments of one's life is to identify the talents which will enable them to achieve their purpose.

In the words of Mark Twain, "The two greatest days of your life are the days you were born and the day you find out why."[7]

Remember, only two percent of the population will ever reach this level according to Simple Psychology.[8] Be the teacher that inspires their students to find their purpose and live a life of self-actualization. By nonverbally communicating the ultimate teacher descriptors, you can be that teacher.

What is the ultimate goal of education in terms of the students?

This was one of the three questions that this book intended to answer. In my opinion, the education of a child should be part of the empowering process of life that helps each student obtain self-actualization.

PUT IT INTO ACTION

What would be (or are) your strategies to help kids in their education who may not have their physiological needs met at home?

If you have achieved self-actualization, who in your life played a prominent role in empowering you to achieve this?

What are some strategies found in the book that will help you become a part of your students hopefully achieving self-actualization?

Social and Emotional Learning

"Social and emotional learning is the process through which children and adults understand and manage their emotions, set and achieve positive goals, feel and show empathy for others, establish and maintain positive relationships, and make responsible decisions."[1]

According to CASEL, there are five core competencies in social and emotional learning:

SELF-AWARENESS

The ability to accurately recognize one's own emotions, thoughts, and values and how they influence behavior. The ability to accurately assess one's strengths and limitations, with a well-grounded sense of confidence, optimism, and a "growth mindset."

SELF-MANAGEMENT

The ability to successfully regulate one's emotions, thoughts, and behaviors in different situations – effectively managing stress, controlling impulses, and motivating oneself. The ability to set and work toward personal and academic goals.

SOCIAL AWARENESS

The ability to take the perspective of and empathize with others, including those from diverse backgrounds and cultures. The ability to understand social and ethical norms for behavior and to recognize family, school, and community resources and supports.

RELATIONSHIP SKILLS

The ability to establish and maintain healthy and rewarding relationships with diverse individuals and groups. The ability to communicate clearly, listen well, cooperate with others, resist inappropriate social pressure, negotiate conflict constructively, and seek and offer help when needed.

RESPONSIBLE DECISION-MAKING

The ability to make constructive choices about personal behavior and social interactions based on ethical standards, safety concerns, and social norms. The realistic evaluation of consequences of various actions, and a consideration of the well-being of oneself and others.[2]

An excellent resource for integrating SEL skills in the classroom can be found at https://www.positiveaction.net/#Home.

"Social-emotional learning helps children develop positive self-esteem, manage their emotions, set and achieve goals, show empathy for others, and handle stress."[3]

The article found on "How to Integrate Social-Emotional Learning (SEL) in the Classroom?" continues with seven strategies on how to teach SEL skills:

1. **Help students identify their self-concept.** This is empowered when you inspire kids to "believe" in who they are. Making your first classroom rule "Always Believe in Yourself" and using the nonverbal skills taught in this book to inspire the kids can empower you to help the kids do this step.

2. **Introduce positive actions for body and mind.** "Educators can introduce positive actions for intellectual health during any subject by encouraging problem solving and creative thinking."[4] A huge goal of my class also involves giving time so the students can teach each other. When kids learn from each other this only empowers their problem-solving skills.

3. **Teach students to manage their feelings and their resources.** "Integrating SEL skills in the classroom includes teaching students how to manage not just their thoughts, feelings, and actions, but also their: time; energy; possessions; money; and talents. Strategies to teach responsibility could include giving them assignments with multiple components that need to be completed by a deadline, asking questions to get them thinking about their feelings and reactions to events, and give them opportunities handle money in the school."[5]

4. **Teach Empathy** - This is done primarily through role-modeling. If you are nonverbally communicating "gentleness" as mentioned in this book, you are likely teaching empathy.

5. **Teach students to face the truth**. Kids need to know when they make errors and learn of their own strengths and weaknesses. By giving students time to work in groups they can learn how to problem solve together and also acknowledge the strengths and weaknesses they and their peers have.

6. **Help students practice self-improvement strategies**. "Once students recognize their weaknesses and learn to own up to their mistakes, they can focus on self-improvement. A growth mindset, or understanding that everyone can learn new skills, plays a key role in knowing how to successfully implement SEL. Teachers at this phase of integrating social-emotional learning in the classroom should help students identify, set, track, and achieve goals. These goals could be related to academics, personal behavior, or physical and mental health."[6]

7. **Review all aspects**. "An important thing that teachers should remember is the Thoughts-Actions-Feelings (TAF) Circle. Positive thoughts lead to positive actions, which lead to positive feelings, which, in turn, create more positive thoughts."[7]

THIS PARALLELS MY POSITIVITY-JOY CYCLE.

If you are continually positive day in and day out, the impact of teaching SEL skills to your students will be a powerful force in your classroom.

Through my experiences of non-verbally communicating love, joy, kindness, patience, peace, goodness, and gentleness to my students, I am indirectly teaching these social and emotional learning competencies. When you reach the point where peace is prevalent in your classroom, most if not all of the five SEL competencies are present in your room. Your role-modeling of gentleness, the ability to show empathy, and patience, the ability to restrain your actions to produce a desired outcome, indirectly teaches children that they too can resolve conflicts and disagreements without using hostility, but through their love of each other. When you combine the non-verbal communication skills with the first rule of *Always Believe in Yourself,* you can be propelling your students to self-awareness and self-management. When kids learn to believe in who they are they can begin the pathway to a growth mindset. They realize through your inspiration that they can achieve the academic goals of your room. Angela's letter below is also a testimony to this.

"Dear Mr. Toups,
Thank you for being such a wonderful and influencing teacher. I will
never forget all the things you taught me. So, when I go to college, I will
still remember my 8ᵗʰ grade math teacher who showed me that he cared
and that if I believe in myself I can do anything!
P.S. Always Believe!!!
—Angela"

This student letter is just one of dozens that I have received that show the non-verbal communication of the ultimate teacher descriptors that teaches kids to learn that they "can." Inspiring a child to *Always Believe* encompasses more than the self-actualization of this; it goes much broader. When a child learns to believe in who they are, the lessons of that moment have far-reaching consequences. The child realizes the world is more than just their needs. The SEL competencies become evident in their life.

When a teacher is using nonverbal communication skills to teach love, joy, kindness, peace, patience, goodness, and gentleness they can not only indirectly inspire their students to *Always Believe in Yourself,* they are also indirectly teaching the five SEL competencies and even possibly inspiring their kids to obtain self-actualization in Maslow's hierarchy of needs. **These lessons, which are not taught, but role modeled and non-verbally communicated, are the greatest lessons that can be taught in the education of a child.**

PUT IT INTO ACTION

What is your takeaway on incorporating teaching SEL skills in your classroom?

What ways mentioned in this chapter could you start teaching in the next class day?

What are some benefits to the kids who are taught SEL skills that may not have been mentioned in this chapter?

Can you think of a teacher that taught you SEL skills?

What did this educator do that made them empower you in your SEL skills?

Mount Rushmore Moment Three

❧

E arlier in the book, you read about two of the Mount Rushmore days of my career. The first of these days happened during the spring of my first year teaching. The dots of my childhood and college life were connected in a powerful way. From that moment forward I knew my "it" in life. I knew my "why." The next moment happened at a GT update in-service in which the presenter told me I had profound nonverbal communication skills, and this is why I was able to inspire kids to "Always Believe." This moment and the resulting reflection of my career led to the writing of this book.

The third Mount Rushmore moment happened when I had an encounter with a former student. One of the great moments of being in education is seeing your former students long after you have been blessed to have them as a student—to hear the stories of how the moments you had with them stayed with them. What truly impacted their lives? Sad to say, but it is usually NOT anything about your academic goals. It was the special moments you created in your classroom that had a lasting impact. It is also the words they describe you with from your non-verbal communication (the theme of this book). If your kids are describing you with the ultimate teacher descriptors, your impact will likely remain with them.

The following is a great example of how being positive each day and doing your best to role model the ultimate teacher descriptors can truly have a lasting impact and change for the better the lives of the kids you are teaching. This story is found in my book, *The Story of Always Believe*, and is called "Don't Stop Believing."

I have videoed myself reading this story. Watching this video is a powerful way to convey the message.

"The Story of Always Believe - Don't Stop Believing"

To summarize this story, I was teaching a sixteen-year-old eighth-grade boy who had a challenging home life situation. Each day during that year, he would usually misbehave. My patience was tested. This boy was probably one of the worst-behaved students I have ever taught. At the end of the year I often envisioned his future and worried what might become of him. I truly thought I had failed this young man and that his future was not going to turn out well.

Years later, I was working at a fundraiser for my church. We were selling pumpkins for Halloween. A young couple entered the area with a precious girl toddler (about two-years-old). The young man came up to me and asked me if I was Mr. Toups. He gave me a hug and told me who he was. It was indeed the 16-year-old eighth grader who had made my life miserable for a whole year. He told me that he never forgot my first rule and that he kept believing. He dropped out of high school but returned and got his GED and was currently an apprentice in a welding program. Once he finished this, he was going to propose to the young lady, and he promised me he would be a better father to his daughter than what he had.

Most educators don't get the opportunity to have a moment like this. Watch the video that is linked, and you might need a tissue to wipe away the tears.

This moment is a tremendous testimony to the power of the words in this book. When you are role-modeling and nonverbally communicating the ultimate teacher descriptors, your influence on the kids in your room is powerful. You may not reach every kid in all your classes, but you may be planting seeds that come to fruit years later.

We are all unique individuals, and we will all convey and role-model the ultimate teacher descriptors in our own unique way. Will we reach one hundred percent of our students each year? The answer is no. Remember our students are all unique individuals. One educator may not reach a child, but in another classroom, another teacher may be having an impact with them, and yet they are both doing their best. We all interact with one another and with our students in unique ways. Keep doing your best to love each student unconditionally, just the way they are, and even though you may not reach every student in the year you teach them, you may reach them years later, just as I was blessed to have the experience in the story "Don't Stop Believing."

PUT IT INTO ACTION

What is one unique way you can relate to kids to plant seeds that might inspire them in the future, even if they are unwilling to learn in the year you teach them?

Mount Rushmore Moment Four

CAREER EQUATES INTO VIDEO DOCUMENTARY

May 2018

Ding. Ding. Ding. Ding. The seventh period dismissal bell ends yet another day of my career. I stand by the door, pat my kids on the back as they leave and tell each student, "You are awesome." The students, as they do each period, leave my room smiling. As the last student walked out the door, I entered my classroom, which is my happy place. Life is so good when I have students in my room. I do my best to make each day an experience that produces a smile on a kid's face and encourages them to "Always Believe" as they master yet another math topic. The experience of my classroom was positive enough that one year one of my students wrote a note to me which said, "Mr. Toups, you make math tolerable."

I walk over to my desk to get my end of the day quiet time. At this time I reflect on my day, things I could have done better, and the needs of some of my students whom I know are struggling, not just in my class, but maybe in life itself. About 15 minutes after dismissal, a young lady walked into my room. "Mr. Toups, hello, my name is Carly Jacobs. How are you doing?"

Carly had an amazing smile, and she certainly had charisma. Her presence made me smile, and I responded with my calling card, "I am AWEsome."

We shook hands. I did not teach this young lady, but I could tell she was interested in seeking something from me. She continued, "Next year is going to be my senior year, and I would love to have your permission to do my video journalism project about how you make the students always believe." She pointed to my "Always Believe Wall" as she said this.

About four years ago my wife gave me the idea to start posting my #BelieveSelfies of the students in my room. When a student gets their selfie on this wall, it is a big event of their high school days. At the end of the year I will cut out all the pictures, sign the back and give them back to the kids.

"You want to do a video documentary about my career?" I asked. I was honored and humbled. How many educators have a career that can be turned into a video documentary?

Carly continued, "Mr. Toups, you are such an enthusiastic teacher. Everyone at school knows who you are. My friends that have had you as a teacher talk so highly of you. I think the story of your career and how you make kids always believe would result in an award-winning video documentary. It is my number one goal to take this project all the way to the state final contest, the Young Filmmakers Festival held in Austin each spring."

I was flabbergasted. What an amazing moment!

"I will help you achieve this goal in any way I can," I told her.

We traded e-mails, and she said, "This summer I will be organizing what I would like to interview you about. We will need to video you during a football game, and I will need to interview some of the staff and some of your current and former students. There is so much to do."

I could tell she was beginning to get overwhelmed thinking about everything she needed to do. "We will get it all done, one day at a time. Just let me know when you would like to video the interview with me. I will be very flexible with the time. You are going to do an amazing job." A good teacher just knows which words and actions are the best for each moment. My smile and words helped calm her down. "Thanks, so much, Mr. Toups. We will be in touch." We shook hands, and she left the room.

The school year ended, and summer began. Carly did not contact me at all. Then once school started up again in August, Carly once again appeared in my room after the seventh period dismissal bell.

"I hope you have had a great summer, Mr. Toups." Carly seemed enthusiastic and upbeat. She had a wonderful smile, and her eyes were twinkling with happiness.

"I am glad to hear from you again, Carly. I hope you have begun to work out what you want to have in your project. Let me know if there is anything I could do to help you out." I was doing my best to reflect her amazing attitude.

"I guess we first need to do the interview. After the interview, I can figure out what we can use. I am limited to only seven minutes in the final project, but I have been taught it is better to have too much material than not enough." I could sense Carly's brain was twirling with what she wanted to include in the video.

"Let me know what day you would like to do the video and I will make it happen." I smiled as I was engaging in the conversation.

"I will figure out when I can get the equipment from journalism then we can plan a date." Carly was always thinking ahead.

"That's fine. You are going to do a great job." I continued to be positive.

"I will get back with you soon and we can set a date to do the initial interview. Could we do it in your classroom?" Carly was still thinking about all that needed to be done.

"That would be fantastic. This is where I feel most comfortable talking about my job." I was trying to accommodate anything that Carly wanted to do.

"Thanks, Mr. Toups. I can't wait to get all this together." Carly smiled as she turned around and left my room.

SEPTEMBER 20, 2018: THE INTERVIEW

The date arrived for the after-school interview. Carly and another student came in and started setting up the equipment for the interview process that featured the Always Believe wall as the background for the interview.

Carly then said, "Mr. Toups, I think we are ready. If you could sit on the desk and answer the questions, that would be great."

I tried to smile as much as I could as she started asking me the questions.

Earlier I gave her an advanced copy of my book *The Story of Always Believe*, and she followed along with the storyline of the book in formulating her questions.

She asked questions about my childhood, being bullied, the incident involving my father, how I became a teacher, the story behind my involvement with Friday Night Lights, special moments I have had with my current and former students, and how I was able to inspire my kids to Always Believe since 1990 when my teaching career began. The interview lasted about an hour.

At the end, she said, "This was fantastic, Mr. Toups. This is exactly what I need to get started." Carly was ecstatic on how I was able to answer the questions in the interview.

"I'm happy this went well. If you have more questions or need to redo anything, let me know. You are going to do a wonderful job." I continued to be upbeat about this process, letting her know I had complete faith in her.

OCTOBER 4, 2018: FRIDAY NIGHT LIGHTS GEORGE RANCH VS ALIEF HASTINGS

October 4, 2018: George Ranch had a home game, and Carly decided on this night to record me in action while I took pictures and videoed the action of the kids performing on the stage that is Texas Friday Night Lights. I started doing this in 2004 and have not missed one game. Seeing the kids perform (not just the football team, the band, drill team, cheerleaders, and the rest of the students) is such a special showcase of the talent that draws me to record the action of as many kids as I can.

Carly interviewed me for a little at the beginning of the game and after halftime, then she was busy interviewing other kids and videoing me. It was a special evening. In the middle of the third quarter, she was standing by me as I was taking selfies with the drill team and other students, and she said "Mr. Toups, your mere presence makes others smile and be happy. You bring out the best of everyone you are by. It is so magical."

After a few more minutes she said, "Mr. Toups, can I get my believe selfie now?"

How could I refuse?

I held the BELIEVE sign in my right hand and with my left hand I held the camera out as far as I could for the selfie. I put on my classic believe selfie smile and snapped a picture of us. Hopefully, this video documentary about my career would be used by other educators to inspire their students to "Always Believe." The picture came out wonderfully, and today it finds a prominent place on the Always Believe wall.

DECEMBER 2019

Carly came by my room after school right before Christmas break. "Mr. Toups, I have got a lot of good videos and I just need some images from our interview." She told me the specific images she needed, *believe* selfies from the game she videoed, a tweet that mentioned a goal of getting a *believe* selfie, and *believe* selfies with specific people.

I replied, "I will get these to you before the holidays. I know this is going to be a great video."

She smiled and said "I hope so, there is still so much to do still. The deadline is January fifteenth."

"You will get it done." I smiled as I spoke. "Just let me know if I can be of any help."

"Thanks, Mr. Toups. You have so much faith in me." She smiled as she turned around and left the room.

JANUARY 9, 2019

About 30 minutes before school started, Carly entered my room with a smile from ear to ear. "Mr. Toups, I finished the video! I hope it meets your approval. I think it is really good."

"When can I see it?" I was so happy she was so positive with her project.

"I will come by after school and we can watch it together. My family has said that it is really good." Her smile did not leave her face.

"It will be hard to go all day long before I can see the video." I was sharing in her happiness.

The final bell finally rang. I dismissed my class and waited anxiously for Carly to come into the room so I could see the video.

Finally, Carly came in. She was glowing with happiness. "Here is the video!" She was holding a flash drive in her hand. "Can we use your display computer?"

Sure, it is already on, just put in the flash drive and open the file."

The Story of Always Believe

The video started playing on the computer, "Always! BELIEVE! Always! BELIEVE!" The video started off with me leading the student body at the October 4 football game in an Always Believe cheer. The video continued with interviews, student testimonies, and my assistant principal giving a testimony on how I impacted my students, school, coworkers, and even community. After seven minutes the video ended dramatically with my #BelieveSelfie wall as the focus.

WOW! I was thinking in my head, she really did a great job! It had professional quality!

I told Carly, "This is amazing! You did an absolutely tremendous job! You should be immensely proud of yourself."

"Do you like it?" She still was not sure.

"It is simply amazing! You did a wonderful job!" I gave her a hug of encouragement.

"If it is ok, I would like to post it on YouTube, but I need your permission," she asked.

"Post it as soon as you can. I am so proud of you."

Carly was smiling ear to ear. "I will upload and post it tonight."

Two evenings later, I pulled up the video on my living room TV and my wife and I watched it together. This was her first time to see it. My wife said, "WOW! This was amazing. Carly did a wonderful job. It is like a professional documentary."

Later that week Carly submitted the video to the UIL Young Filmmakers association for the state contest. Now it was a waiting game.

Two weeks passed and Carly came to my room. "Mr. Toups!" Carly was smiling from ear to ear. "I made the first cut!" There are two more cut-off points until the final projects are selected! I am so excited!"

I gave Carly a hug and shared in her excitement. One of the great moments of an educator's career is seeing the students you are blessed to influence succeed in their dreams. Hopefully the video would at least make it to the state finals.

The following week Carly's journalism teacher, Mrs. Riley, e-mailed me and told me that the video made the next cut. There were 16 projects left and the final eight would make it to the finals. This was all too good to be true.

At the end of February Carly came to my room with tears of joy in her eyes, "Mr. Toups, we made it to the finals! Our video will be shown at the film festival in two weeks!"

It was amazing that she was referring to her project as ours. She was simply an amazing young lady. I was so happy for her.

TUESDAY, MARCH 5, 2019

It was the big day! My wife and I made the 2.5-hour drive to Austin to watch Carly's video at the Texas Young Filmmakers Festival. The event was held in the iconic Paramount Theatre in downtown Austin. The venue was simply beautiful. We found Carly and her family outside the theater and took pictures to commemorate the event.

The contest was divided into Division One and Division Two and then there were several categories: Digital Animation, Documentary, Narrative, and Traditional Animation. The first part of the program consisted of watching all the projects. It was fascinating to see what the students in Texas were producing. Carly's video came on and afterwards a round of applause ensued.

After all the projects were shown, there was an intermission. Outside of the theater, many people recognized me from the video and were asking for #BelieveSelfies. I smiled again and again for the dozens of kids and adults who wanted a picture with the now famous red BELIEVE sign. After the impromptu photo session, Carly's family, Mrs. Riley, and my wife and I walked to a nearby restaurant. During dinner we all agreed that Carly's video had an excellent chance of being one of the top three documentaries.

It was time to head back to the theater for the award ceremonies. My heart was racing. I could only imagine how nervous Carly and her parents were.

The awards started off with the Digital Animation awards. The winners had their video shown and then went onstage to receive their trophies.

After Digital Animation it was our turn.

"The awards for documentary Division One!" The emcee on the stage first presented the Division One smaller schools awards.

Then it was the moment Carly was waiting for.

"In Documentaries Division 2 - Third place, the winner goes to Versatile, by Bel Air High School in El Paso, Texas!" The video played and after the video the class that made the video went on stage to receive their awards.

"The second-place winner is...(there was a pause) *The Story of Always Believe* by Carly from George Ranch High School!" Carly and the rest of us were so happy! We quietly watched the video play again, then Carly went on stage to receive her award. While she was on stage, the emcee asked her to come over. They talked and then she pointed toward where we were sitting.

The emcee then said, "How about Mr. Toups? Come on stage to share this moment." There was thunderous applause from the audience. This moment was all about Carly and to be able to join her on stage WAS the greatest Mount Rushmore moment of my teaching career. I got on stage and the lady handing out the trophies shook my hand and said, "It is such an honor to be able to meet you. The video is simply amazing."

I smiled and said, "Thank you."

Then I walked over to the emcee. He put his hand on my shoulder and said, "Thank you for the thousands of kids in your career that have been impacted by what you do. It is an honor to be able to meet you. I am so glad you are here with Carly."

Carly and I walked backstage and got official pictures for the UIL.

The rest of the event was a blur. I was walking on air for the rest of the time just soaking in this moment. The awards and finalists can be found at this web page.

UIL 2019 FINALISTS:
https://www.uiltexas.org/2019-finalists-and-results-with-links-to-films

 After the event, there was another round of students and adults wanting to get #BelieveSelfies with, "the famous Mr. Toups." The moment you become a celebrity at an event like this is truly life touching. This event was all about showcasing the talents of our kids, but my life story and Carly's documentary about it was highlighting the evening. The image to the left is just one example of the happiness and smiles that getting a picture with me and that famous red BELIEVE sign produced that evening.

Can your career as an educator produce a documentary?

A career that can produce a documentary is not about awards or honors acquired by a teacher, but it is all about the words the kids use to describe who you are.

PUT IT INTO ACTION

I have had many goals and dreams come true as an educator. These dreams came true because I "believed" and walked the talk. What is a career goal or dream you would like to write down?

Closing Thoughts

If someone walked into your classroom after school hours and looked at the material on your classroom walls, what would they say about you?

Just my opinion—your classroom walls should be a showcase of student work, tell your story, and hopefully a display of your learning objectives. My walls are lined with student work and posters that I made from my own pictures. I also have a "Mr. Toups Meme of the Week" that is posted. Last year one of my students told me, "Mr. Toups, you are the only 'meme-able' teacher I have ever had."

One year I was giving a benchmark test in my room. The kids were alpha split, so I had students in my room that I didn't teach. While we were waiting for the principal to give the go ahead for testing, the students were looking around my room and absorbing all the phrases and pictures. One of the kids then said, "How can you sit in this room and not be inspired?"

Here are some of my top inspirational posters and memes.

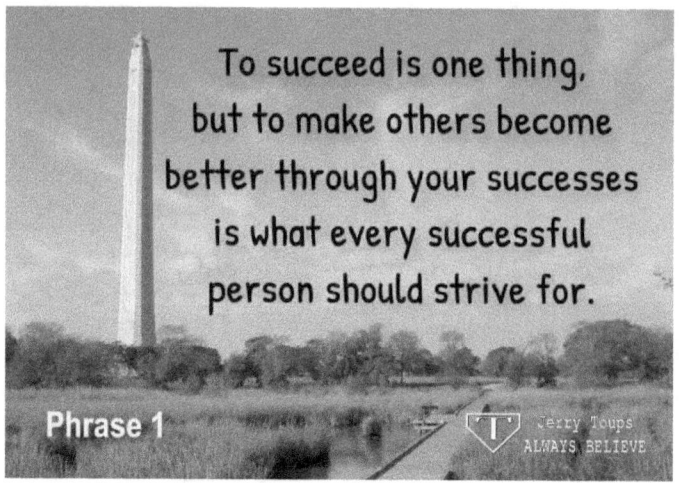

To succeed is one thing, but to make others become better through your successes is what every successful person should strive for.

Phrase 1

Jerry Toups
ALWAYS BELIEVE

On the first day of school I have a journal that contains the phrases I have written and some of the original manuscripts of the stories that are in my first book, *The Story of Always Believe*. I pointed out this phrase to the students on day one and told them this was the beginning of my writing, which eventually led me to becoming an author. I also share with them that I never made an "A" in English, yet I "believed" enough that I wrote a book good enough to get published.

The only classroom rule I have posted in my room is "Always Believe In Yourself." To reroute behavior for the greater good of learning and to effectively manage my classroom behavior, I have a few posters I point to when students make errors in their behavior. Many times, the kids will self-correct each other and call out these "rules."

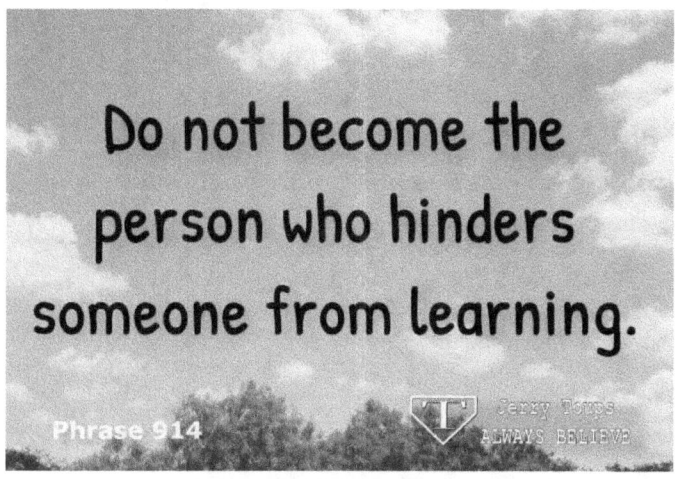

This phrase pretty much sums up all the classroom rules you can write with one poster. If students start behaving to where it is impacting the learning of their peers, I just point to this poster which is on the front wall of my classroom. This is usually all it takes to get the kids back on task.

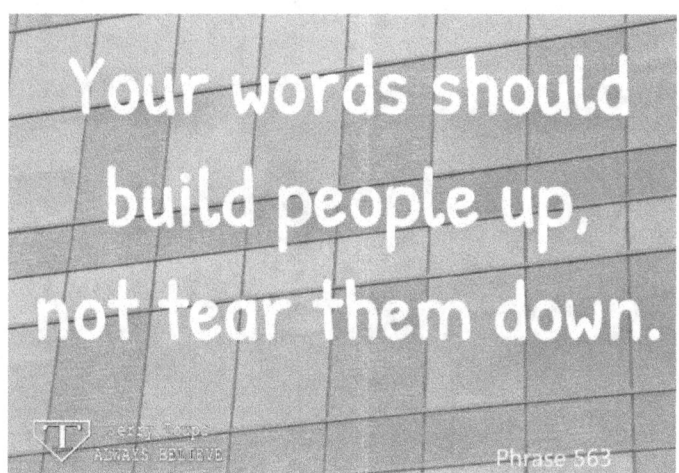

In today's world of anti-bullying, this poster is huge. My classroom is a positive haven. When kids begin talking negatively about others, I just point to this poster. This also involves the teacher role-modeling this phrase. Your words should not tear down groups of people.

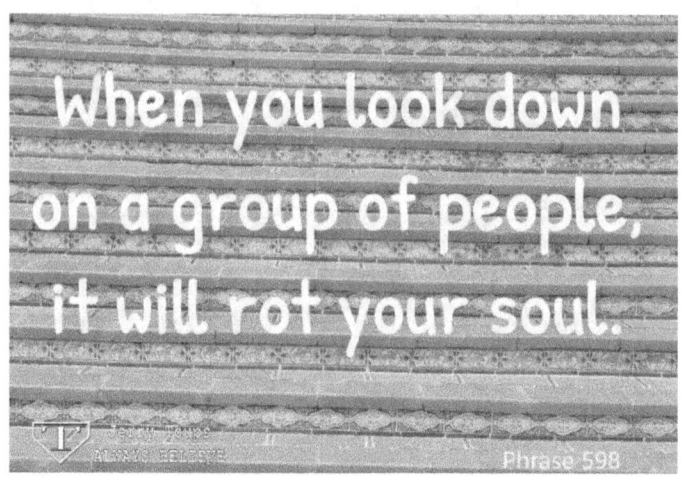

When you look down on a group of people, it will rot your soul.

Phrase 598

This is also a powerful phrase to show kids that you should not judge a group of people. This is role modeled by my words. Teach kids to judge each other individually on their skills and character.

Those who complain often will soon become the complaint of others.

Phrase 103

This poster pretty much eliminates any complaining in my room. The kids do not hear me complain about items related to my job or the current events. When you enable kids to complain about things, it will fester and take away the positive vibe you should be building in your room.

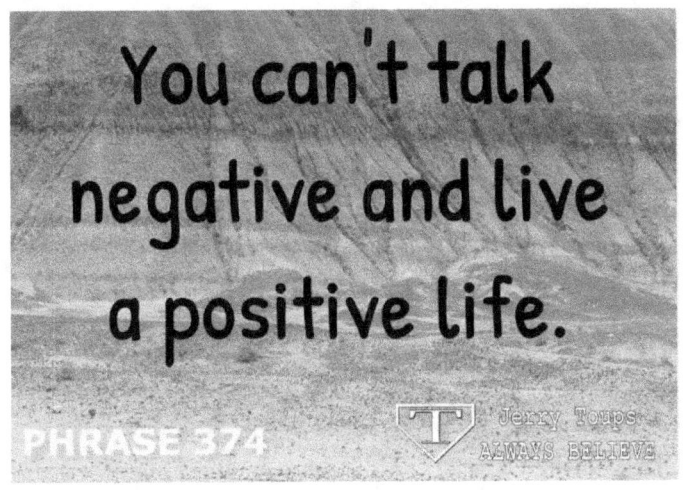

Role model what it means to be positive. Tell them the attributes of being positive. When negative comments are made, point to this poster.

The following posters are inspirational posters for kids to read and strive to achieve.

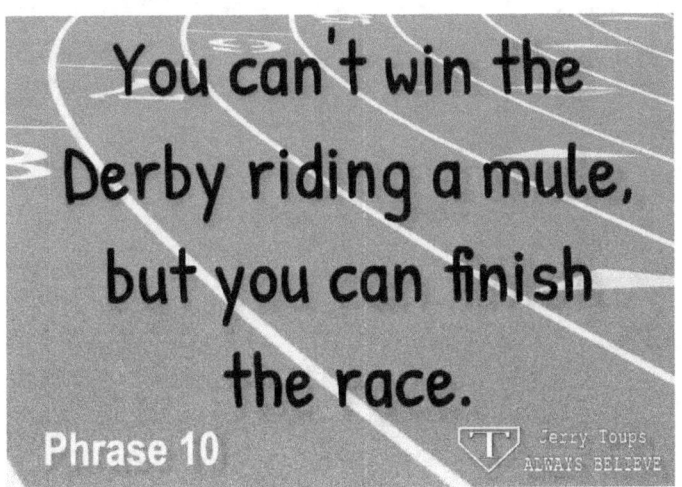

This poster is a classic example of "grit" —of NOT GIVING UP! Let the kids know it is ok to fall short. That sometimes you will be facing people with greater resources or talents. ALWAYS finish the race.

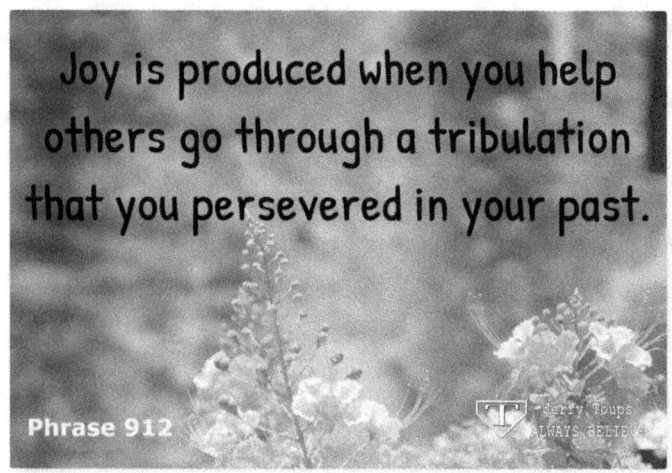

Joy is produced when you help others go through a tribulation that you persevered in your past.

Phrase 912

Jerry Toups
ALWAYS BELIEVE

Kids need to know their tribulations can eventually be a powerful generator of joy. Tell the kids of your childhood tribulations. Let them know you have been there and done that.

Love for others based on their actions to make you happy is doomed to failure.

Inspired Phrase 678

Jerry Toups
ALWAYS BELIEVE

This is a truth for kids going through puppy love and the devastating moments of teenage heartbreak. Do not love someone to make you happy. Do not let your happiness be based on whether you have a boyfriend or girlfriend.

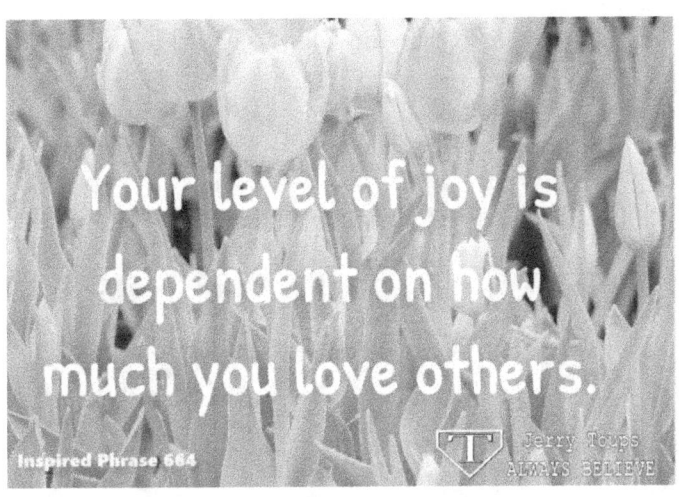

Your level of joy is dependent on how much you love others.

Inspired Phrase 664

Jerry Toups
ALWAYS BELIEVE

Loving others produces joy. This joy is priceless. When you love the kids and the kids know they are loved just the way you are, the joy that is produced will be felt in your room.

Your radiant beauty is increased as you make your heart purer.

Jerry Toups
ALWAYS BELIEVE

Phrase 579

Students need to see this. Tell the kids that beauty from within over-powers physical beauty. Tell the kids to love who they are and what they look like. Every human is different. We are not all built to be magazine cover models. When this is role modeled to your kids, they will be more self-confident of who they are.

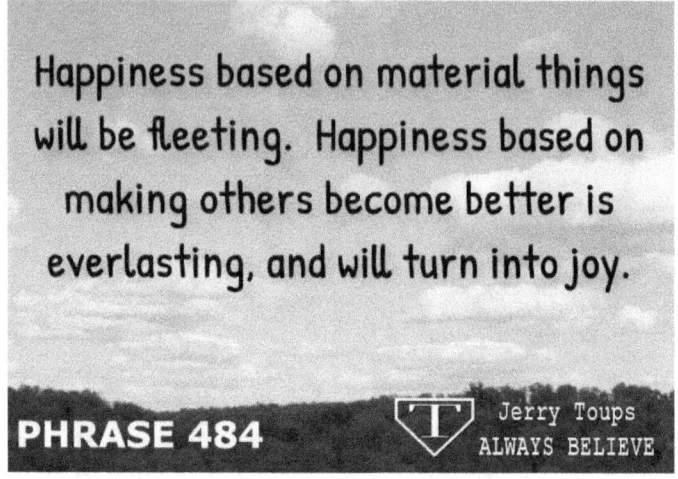

In our material world, the kids need to hear this. Let them know that material things will only develop greed and the desire to have more. Role model what it means to make others better.

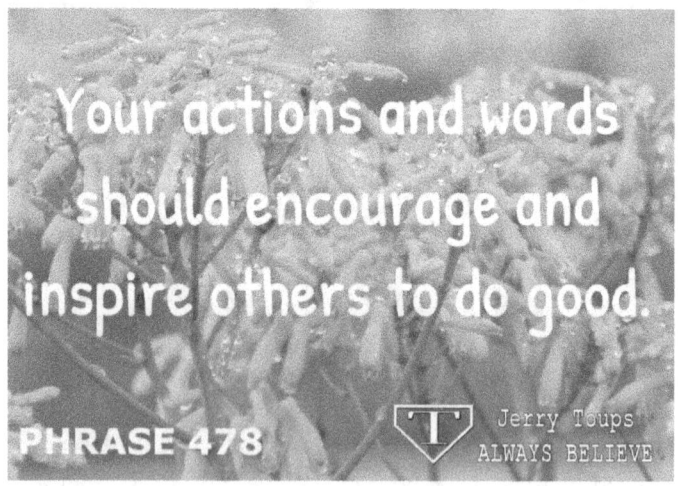

Kids need to realize their actions and words do indeed have an impact on those around them. Let them know this truth. When kids become aware of the impact they are having on others you can change their actions to being a force of good instead of bad.

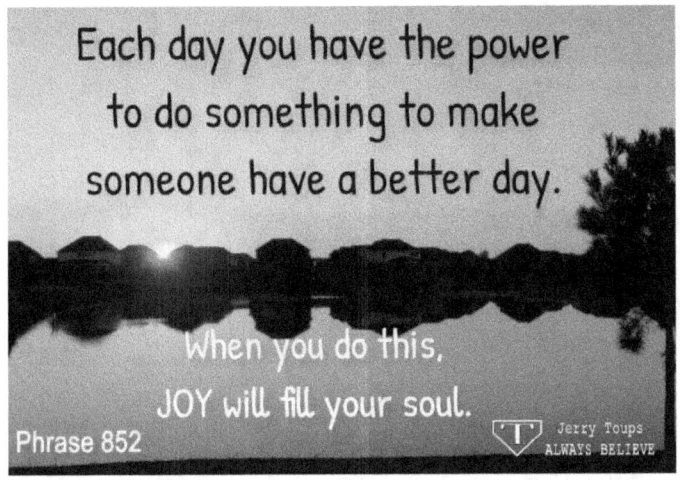

If there was one truth I could wish that my students would grow up and do it would be this phrase. Role model random acts of kindness to all your students. Try to encourage your students to show random acts of kindness to their peers. This is a life lesson that will have a great impact on the future of your community.

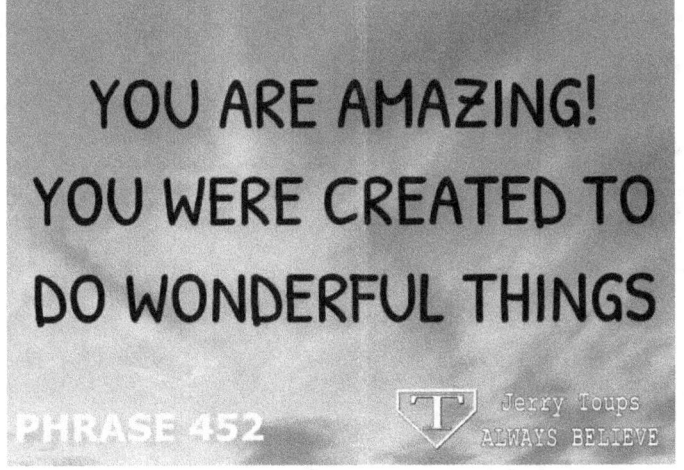

Every kid in every school throughout this country should be told this every day. Every kid needs to hear they will do wonderful things. This is a huge truth that will enable them to Always Believe in who they are.

The following posters are some of my most-liked memes.

This was the very first #ToupsPose taken by my wife. It is from the summit of High Point in New Jersey. Do a search for #toupspose on Twitter or Instagram to view these pictures.

This was taken at the beach at San Simeon California: an all-time epic #ToupsPose.

These are two of my most popular Mr. Toups memes. The kids love it when I make a meme with me smiling that gives them a smile. Sometimes just by seeing these memes, I give the student one of the best moments of their day.

The following student letters were written in the shortened school year of 2019-2020. Due to the COVID-19 virus my school district went on Spring Break vacation and did not return. The letters continue to provide testimony to the power of non-verbal communication skills found in this book. As you read through these letters, write down the ultimate teacher descriptors (love, joy, kindness, peace, patience, goodness, gentleness, and positivity) that can be found in each letter.

"Mr. Toups, I would like to say thank you for all the times you let us have fun and enjoy the class. Thank you for always interacting with us in fun ways, whether it was reading us your stories or your funny sounds. You showed me the fun in learning, and easier ways to learn math. This was one of my favorite classrooms because you always believed in us and inspired us with your quotes and all the activities we did. I truly wish these

moments did not end like this, but I will never forget the class and the help you gave me. You will be missed but never forgotten!"
—Sheryl

"I would like to say thank you because you have truly made learning fun and easy for me this year. I am not the greatest at math, but this year I feel like I for once actually knew what I was doing in the class. Thank you for being a fun teacher just to make the school day feel happier in between other stressful classes.
—Megan

"Goodbye, Mr. Toups. I had so much fun being one of your students this year. Not only did you help me really understand and succeed in algebra, but you put a smile on my face and made me laugh every single day. I will never forget you and will most definitely come visit you next fall. Have a wonderful summer Mr. Toups and thank you for everything you have done. I will never stop believing."
—Kevin

"I just wanted to say how much you have inspired me to better myself and others. You are truly a blessing and have changed my life for the better. You are the best math teacher I've ever received, and I just wanted to tell you thank you. Any student that has you is blessed to have you. <3"
—Alicia

"Bye, I will miss your positivity."
—Ashlyn

"Dear Mr. Toups,
I will miss your great classroom environment and your creative ways of teaching!
Thank you for being an AWESOME teacher!"
—Erica

"Dear Mr. Toups. I loved being a student of yours because you taught me to always believe no matter what. You are so positive and always making everyone around you happy. I will miss you next year!
—Belinda

"I will miss having you as a teacher. I will miss having a person that will always ha[s] energy even if he feels sick. Someone who doesn't let anyone make them change character no matter who he is. I know I have not been the best student behaviorally but still did well academically because of you and for that I am so much grateful. Being able to spend my first high school year with you was the most fun math class ever and I will never forget it. Love you dawg. See you next year.
—Michaal

"Mr. Toups, you were my favorite teacher. You genuinely made class a fun learning experience. You made me laugh and smile on my worst days. You always inspire me to keep moving forward and to believe. In your class I had lots of fun. I wish I could have you next year too. I am genuinely going to miss coming to class and see you there. Keep inspiring the future classes to come. Love you, Mr. Toups"
—Philip

"Thank you for always having our best interest at heart and your love for teaching always shined through, you were a really great teacher whose love for his students showed!"
—Cali

∾

These student letters are testimony to the following inspired phrases that I have written.

Great teachers form relationships whose lessons last a lifetime.

A teacher's role modeling of love, kindness, peace, patience, goodness, gentleness, and joy is a lesson that their student will remember far longer than their academic objectives.

When teachers love their students for who they are, joy will fill their heart and contentment will rule their actions. They will be able to overlook student misbehavior as foolish actions and guide them to proper actions.

Teachers should leave footprints in their student's heart that endure for a lifetime.

The impact of a teacher should give their students hope for their future.

True genuine praise given to others consistently over time will turn you into a beacon of hope.

Hopefully after reading this book as an educator, you will realize that the nonverbal communication skills you are showing your students far exceeds the academic knowledge you have on the subject matter. You cannot expect kids to sit and get day after day. You may be a member of MENSA in your subject knowledge, but if you cannot manage the behavior of the kids, you will not be successful as an educator. As illustrated in this book, when you manage your kid's behavior through love and the other descriptors, your classroom will become magical. Yet, how many workshops or teacher in-services have you been to that teaches you how to nonverbally communicate to the kids. It has been said that kids do not learn from teachers they do not like, yet as educators we are not taught how to love the kids for who they are. We are told to love the kids and form relationships, and that is usually where this wisdom stops. We are not shown how to form these relationships. When the students in your class begin doing what is correct in your room through following the examples you set with them, instead of following structured rules and fear of not following them, your relationships with the kids will have another dimension. The kids are far more likely to remember the example of you walking the talk over your enforcement of a set of procedures. The relationships that change lives are created by the moments when you are role-modeling the ultimate teacher descriptors. The moments created by these relationships are what your kids will remember. The inspiration you generate from role modeling the ultimate teacher descriptors has the potential to change the lives of those around you.

On the following page you will copy the words you wrote following each section on how you will role-model and nonverbally communicate the ultimate teacher descriptors. On the flip side of the page are my words on how I have done this since the beginning of my career in 1990. Read through this page each day. Create times to have your reflection and quiet time are when you get to school, during lunch, and at the end of your day when you are about to pack up and leave. By reading through your words daily you are likely to start reproducing the actions that nonverbally communicate the descriptors.

ULTIMATE TEACHER DESCRIPTORS

LOVE

KINDNESS

FAITHFULNESS

GENTLENESS

GOODNESS

PATIENCE

PEACE

JOY
(Write down the phrases of how joy is generated that you marked.)

ULTIMATE TEACHER DESCRIPTORS
#AlwaysBelieve

LOVE
The unconditional actions of putting the needs of others ahead of your own.

KINDNESS
Actions showing the goodness of your heart regardless of what others do.

FAITHFULNESS
When your actions are true to your words

GENTLENESS
The opposite of harshness. Being careful with your student's feelings.

GOODNESS
Character recognized in quality or conduct. The best part of anything.

PATIENCE
Your ability to restrain your actions to produce good.

PEACE
The state of contentment generated from knowing your actions are pure.

JOY
The inner-being generated state of happiness others can sense.

POSITIVITY

How do you feel when you are around someone who is positive? What do positive people do so you know they are positive?	How would you create a positive environment in your classroom? Be specific.
What is one thing you will do to create a positive experience on the first day of school?	What are ways you can positively affect your school community?

Once you have completed filling in the previous pages, make copies of them and read through them each day. Make it a habit to have quiet and or reflection time each day. This might be the most profound three to five minutes of your day. Focus on the descriptors and how to reproduce them. Looking back at my career, these descriptors have become a way of life for me. I naturally nonverbally communicate the descriptors. This comes through years of reflection time.

I would like to add, your practice of patience is perhaps the greatest descriptor produced from your love of the kids. You must have patience in your room. One negative snap can destroy the actions you are trying to build. Kids are likely not to forget the times you snap or the negative moments that are generated from your actions. This happens when your patience fails you. The power of one negative memory is tenfold the power of a happy memory. One sentence spoken in anger can wipe out your influence on the kids for the rest of the year. Once you say something you cannot unsay it. Be slow to speak. A single word can undo a lifetime of love. This is usually the downfall for many educators. Your self-care is essential to your patience. Make sure you are doing things you like during your off-school hours. If you are not doing this, you will burn out.

As mentioned, there are not many how-to books written on inspiration, because we are all unique individuals teaching unique children. There is no "one way" to replicate inspiration with an "inspire meter." The continued studies into mirror neurons should be fascinating and worthy of your time. If these studies start to become replicated, it will detail how we think and feel as humans and using this knowledge we can continue to get ways to become educators who inspire kids.

During the course of my blessed career I have lived to see many of my dreams and goals become reality. I can truly say that in my career I am living the dream by going to work each day. Having the opportunity to write this book with EduMatch is just another example of living the dream. My dream now is that some school will make the step to become an #AlwaysBelieve school. All the classrooms would use Always Believe in Yourself as the first rule. The teachers would be made aware of how they as individuals can nonverbally replicate the ultimate teacher descriptors. The school would become part of the student's lifelong path to self-actualization. Teaching SEL skills would become part of the daily instruction of the teachers through nonverbally communicating the ultimate teacher descriptors. Children would begin to believe in who they are and would realize they were created to do wonderful things.

I would like to close this book with the importance you have over the kids that are in your class and in your school. Your influence can go beyond the walls of your school through the nonverbal communication of the ultimate teacher descriptors. The more you invest in the life of others the greater your life becomes. Make your life about loving the kids that you are blessed to see. Why do you do what you do? If it is about you, your life will have less meaning, if it is about others, your life will be full and meaningful.

Your relationships with others will flourish when you become one that others desire to be around. If the people in your life are describing who you are with the descriptors found in this book, you will build relationships that change the future. Your life as an educator can truly turn into a legacy when you role model the descriptors. You can have an impact not just on the kids in your classroom, but on the school community. Child by child you can change the world for the better.

God bless & <3 Mr. Toups.

Bibliography

Opening
1 Lorre, C (Writer), & Cendrowski, M (Director). (2009, March 2). The Cushion Saturation (Season 2 Episode 16) [TV series episode] C Lorre, B Prady (Executive Producers) *The Big Bang Theory*. CBS

Intrinsic vs Extrinsic
1 Lorre, C, Aronsohn, L, Reynolds, J (Writers), & Cendrowski, M (Director). (2011, February 3). The Thespian Catalyst (Season 4 Episode 14) [TV series episode] C Lorre, B Prady (Executive Producers) *The Big Bang Theory*. CBS
2 Bhandari, S., Yadav, P., Yadav, C. (n.d.) *Difference Between Intrinsic and Extrinsic Motivation*. Retrieved August 1, 2021, from https://askanydifference.com/ru/difference-between-intrinsic-and-extrinsic-motivation/
3 IBID
4 Deci, E., & Ryan, R. (January 28, 2018) *Intrinsic Motivation in Psychology*, https://www.explorepsychology.com/intrinsic-motivation-psychology/
5 IBID

Always Believe
1 Shorten, A. (n.d.) *How To Believe In Yourself Using Positive Thinking*. Retrieved August 1, 2021, from https://www.thelawofattraction.com/believe-in-yourself/
2 IBID
3 Robbins, T. (n.d.) *11 Ways to Believe in Yourself*. Retrieved August 1, 2021, from https://www.tonyrobbins.com/building-confidence/how-to-believe-in-yourself/
4 Ross, L (2021, September 21) *"It's Kind of Fun to Do the Impossible": 4 Lessons on Following Your Dreams from Walt Disney*. https://www.thomasnet.com/insights/lessons-from-leaders-walt-disney/

INSPIRATION
1 Merriam-Webster (n.d.) *Inspire*. Retrieved January 30, 2022 from https://www.merriam-webster.com/dictionary/inspire
2 The Free Dictionary (n.d.) *Inspire*. Retrieved January 30, 2022 from https://www.thefreedictionary.com/inspire

3 Robbins, T. (n.d.) *How to Inspire Others*. Retrieved July 20, 2021 from https://www.tonyrobbins.com/buisness/how-to-inspire-others/

4 IBID

5 IBID

6 Angier, M. (n.d.) *Top Ten Ways To Inspire Others to Be Their Best*. Retrieved July 20, 2021 from www.appleseeds.org/10-inspire_Angier.htm

7 Schwantes, M. (n.d.) *8 Things the Smartest Leaders Do to Motivate Their Employees*. Retrieved July 20, 2021 from https://www.inc.com/marcel-schwantes/8-powerful-ways-to-motivate-inspire-your-employees-this-week.html

8 IBID

9 Holzer, A., Spataro, S., Grace Baron, J., (2019) *Dare to Inspire*.

10 Barrington Irving interview by Allison A. Holzer and Jen Grace Baron, December 10, 2018

11 Holzer, A., Spataro, S., Grace Baron, J., (2019) *Dare to Inspire*.

12 IBID

13 Kaplan, J., & Iacoboni, M., (2006) *Getting a Grip on Other Minds: Mirror Neurons, Intention, Understanding, and Cognitive Empathy*. Social Neuroscience 1, no. 3-4; 175-183

14 Carr, L., Iacoboni, M., Dubeau, M., Mazziotta, J.,& Lenzi G. (2003). *Neural Mechanisms of Empathy in Humans: A relay from Neural Systems for Imitation to Limbic Areas*. Proceedings of the National Academy of Sciences 100, no. 9 5497-5502

15 Peterson, C., Seligman, M., (2004) *Character Strengths and Virtues: A Handbook and Classification*, vol. 1 New York: Oxford University Press

MOUNT RUSHMORE DAY 2

1 Carr, L., Iacoboni, M., Dubeau, M., Mazziotta, J.,& Lenzi G. (2003). *Neural Mechanisms of Empathy in Humans: A relay from Neural Systems for Imitation to Limbic Areas*. Proceedings of the National Academy of Sciences 100, no. 9 5497-5502

NON-VERBAL COMMUNICATION

1 Bailiy, S., Reilly, M., (2016, December 12) *Students Never Forget How You Make Them Feel*. Corwin Connect. https://corwin-connect.com/2016/12/students-never-forget-make-feel/

2 Business Jargons (n.d.) Non-Verbal Communication Retrieved January 30, 2022, from https://businessjargons.com/non-verbal-communication.html

ULTIMATE TEACHER DESCRIPTORS

1 Six Seconds (2012, January 16) *Are We Wired for Empathy*. Six Seconds https://www.6seconds.org/2012/01/16/are-we-wired-for-empathy/

2 IBID

3 IBID

4 IBID

KINDNESS

1 Colins Dictionary (n.d.) *Kindness*. Retrieved January 22, 2022 from https://www.collins dictionary.com/dictionary/english/kindness

FAITHFULNESS

1 Dictionary.com (n.d.) *Faithful*. Retrieved January 22, 2022 from https://www.dictionary. com/browse/faithful

2 Robbins, T. (n.d.) *11 Ways to Believe in Yourself*. Retrieved August 1, 2021 from https:// www.tonyrobbins.com/building-confidence/how-to-believe-in-yourself/

GENTLENESS

1 Merriam Webster (n.d.) *Gentleness*. Retrieved August 4, 2021 from https://www.merriam-webster.com/dictionary/gentleness

2 The Free Dictionary (n.d.) *Gentleness*. Retrieved August 4, 2021 from https://www. thefreedictionary.com/gentleness

3 Dictionay.com (n.d.) *Gentleness*. Retrieved August 4, 2021 from https://www.dictionary. com/browse/gentleness

4 Foster, E (n.d.) *Fruit of the Spirit: Gentleness*. Life Hope & Truth Retrieved August 4, 2021 from https://lifehopeandtruth.com/god/holy-spirit/the-fruit-of-the-spirit/fruit-of-the-spirit-gentleness/

GOODNESS

1 Merriam Webster (n.d.) *Goodness*. Retrieved August 4, 2021 from https://www.merriam-webster.com/dictionary/goodness

2 Dictionary.com (n.d.) *Goodness*. Retrieved August 4, 2021 from https://www.dictionary.com/browse/goodness

PATIENCE

1 bing.com (n.d.) *patience definition*. Retrieved January 30,2022 from https://www.bing. com/search?q=patience&form=QBLH&sp=-1&pq=patien&sc=6-6&qs=n&sk=&cvid= 9876D5117F964E8CBDD836ECED2B93AA

2 The Free Dictionary (n.d.) *patient*. Retrieved January 30, 2022 from https://www.thefreedictionary.com/patient

3 Warren M., Brooks-Gunn J. (1989)., *Mood and behavior at adolescence: evidence for hormonal factors*.PubMed.gov https://pubmed.ncbi.nlm.nih.gov/2525135/

PEACE

1 The Free Dictionary (n.d.) *peace*. Retrieved January 30, 2022 from Peace - definition of peace by The Free Dictionary

2 Merriam Webster (n.d.) *vibe*. Retrieved January 30, 2022 from https://www.merriam-webster.com/dictionary/vibe

3 Bing (n.d.) *vibe definition*. Retrieved January 30, 2022 from

https://www.bing.com/search?q=vibe+definition&form=QBLH&sp=-1&ghc=1&pq=vibe+definition&sc=8-15&qs=n&sk=&cvid=44F609DD366349FA8E2987EB6203E1EF

4 Collins Dictionary (n.d.) *vibe*. Retrieve January 30, 2022 from https://www.collinsdictionary.com/dictionary/english/vibe

JOY

1 Merriam Webster (n.d) *joy*. Retrieved January 30, 2022 from https://www.merriam-webster.com/dictionary/joy

2 Dicionary.com (n.d.) *joy*. Retrieved January 30, 2022 from https://www.dictionary.com/browse/joy

POSITIVE JOY CYCLE

1 Greenfield, R., (2016, January 25) *15 Tips To Be A Positive Influence on Others*. Rob Greenfield https://www.robgreenfield.org/positiveinfluence/

2 Sterling E. (n.d.) *How To Inspire Others? Positive Encouragement Is Key*. ESterling LLC Retrieved January 30, 2022, from https://esterlingllc.com/how-to-inspire/

MASLOW'S HIERARCHY

1 More S., (n.d.) *Maslow's Hierarchy of Needs | What is Maslow's Theory?* Psych Side Retrieved January 30, 2022, from

https://www.psychside.com/maslows-hierarchy-of-needs-what-is-maslows-theory/

2 McLeod, S., (2020, December 29) *Maslow's Hierarchy of Needs*. Simply Psychology.
https://www.simplypsychology.org/maslow.html

3 IBID

4 IBID

5 IBID

6 IBID

7 Woodall, T. (2015, July 22) *qod22*. Goal Getting Post. http://www.goalgettingpodcast.com/qod22/

8 McLeod, S., (2020, December 29) *Maslow's Hierarchy of Needs*. Simply Psychology.
https://www.simplypsychology.org/maslow.html

SEL

1 Casel. (n.d.) *Fundamentals of SEL*. Retrieved January 30, 2022 from,
https://casel.org/what-is-sel/

2 Casel. (n.d.) *What is the CASEL Framework?* Retrieved January 30, 2022 from,
https://casel.org/core-competencies/

3 Positive Action. (2020, August 27). *How to Integrate Social-Emotional Learning (SEL) in the Classroom?*
https://www.positiveaction.net/blog/social-emotional-learning-in-the-classroom

About the Author

From the banks of the Trinity River to those of the Brazos, **Jerry Toups, Jr.** is known as the Jedi of Believe. Whether you were in his class, performing under Friday Night Lights, or just knew of him, the aurora of positivity was always strong. With his #1 rule of "Always Believe in Yourself," Jerry Toups has been teaching students since 1990 the power of believing in themselves and realizing that they are made for awesomeness.

In his first book, *The Story of Always Believe*, Jerry Toups introduced us to how his #1 rule came to be. Now, his goal is to show current and future educators how exhibiting the "Ultimate Teacher Descriptors" of Love, Joy, Peace, Patience, Kindness, Goodness, Faithfulness, and Gentleness will inspire the next generation of believers, who will then inspire the generation after them, and so on. By showing students how to Always Believe, greatness and joy will abound.

In the words of Jerry Toups, Jr., "YOU were created to do WONDERFUL things, and YOU are AWESOME! #AlwaysBelieve!"

Ryan Schuldt
Former Dayton ISD student and current teacher

Jerry Toups, Jr.
Website – www.toupsgraphics.com
YouTube - https://www.youtube.com/user/toupsgraphics
Twitter - @Toups_J
Instagram - tex_toups
Facebook – Jerry Toups